As a new writer the creative games, and co
me the boost I needed, and a confidence I
look back at what I have written and I can

~ Sophia Skyers

Workshops with Vanessa are like little adventures where you're encouraged to explore uncharted territory you thought you'd never dare risk! With professional but good-humoured guidance she leads you down new paths of creativity, skilfully staging the tasks she sets. It's joyous, absorbing, challenging - and fun!

~ Nell Bacon

I'm a massive pontificator, full of ideas but never manage to get going. Attending Vanessa's writing workshops changed all that. Writing games that are imaginative, inventive and original. Definitely designed to get the creative juices flowing.

~ Sarah Fuell

Sometimes in a writer's life, words don't show up: characters don't want to speak, settings refuse to come into full view. Writing games like these give us the chance to write for fun, as quickly as possible, in response to a few words, a photograph, a description of a strange place in the past or future or a world that doesn't really exist. Playing around with words, with a time limit and companions who are also typing or scribbling furiously, reminds us that we can write and that writing can be fun.

~ Frances Hay

Vanessa's workshops empower you to play with words without overthinking. There is a sense of freedom without judgement, but also a quiet acceptance that not every piece of writing will work the first time. Going with the flow sparked new ideas that were completely unexpected... sometimes random...sometimes not even obvious...the workshops have been an enriching and invaluable discovery in my creative process.

~ Maria Sanger

Published by Ad Hoc Fiction.
www.AdHocFiction.com

Purchasing Information:
Paperback available from www.AdHocFiction.com
E-book available from all usual outlets.

Printed in the United Kingdom.
First Printing 2023.

ISBN paperback 978-1-915247-44-5
ISBN e-Book 978-1-915247-45-2

51 AND A HALF

games and ideas for writers with example responses

VANESSA GEBBIE

AdHoc Fiction

For Millie Gebbie, my 12 year old granddaughter who is already a writer,
and will always be a writer whatever else she does.

CONTENTS

PART ONE

WELCOME

Welcome to my little book of writing games, for writers who want to explore fresh ways to open up their writing. Here, you have pages and pages of tried and tested games, and interesting scenarios in which to drop existing characters, or to help you create completely new ones. Not just new characters. New voices. New settings. New everythings.

The technical term is: 'Stuff to stretch you creatively.'

We are all different and respond to stimuli in different ways, and that is how it should be – how boring would it be if we were all the same? And to complicate matters, if you are anything like me, what gets your creativity buzzing on a Monday afternoon might well not work the next morning – so go with the flow, I say. No pressure.

What resources do you need, apart from your imagination, memory, and a pen and paper or laptop? Not a lot. Access to the Internet/Google – such an interesting resource, even if it does need managing. Access to a dictionary – there are plenty online. And that's about it.

Why not dip in and see what appeals today?

I love to work with writing games. From both sides. I love them as a teacher and a sharer of all things writing, as I've seen the results, over and over – and I love using them for my own writing. Games remove the pressure to perform that we carry, all of us, as writers. That pressure doesn't just come from outside us, it becomes an internal thing, too. We can so easily find ourselves in a place where we feel we aren't allowed, so we take our eye off the ball of whatever project we are working on. "Mustn't. Have to concentrate." But here, you are absolutely encouraged to break that "Mustn't". That's why I am more comfortable calling them games, ideas, because they are intended to be fun. And unless we can play now and again, and loosen our creative constraints, doesn't our writing become sticky?

Most of these are self-explanatory, but where necessary, I'll explain how I came up with that idea or who I credit for the inspiration. I'll also show you how you can apply the same processes to your own exercises, if you would like to try them out on your writing group, for example.

And finally, the results. Some lovely, generous writers have sent me the writing they did in workshops, in many cases their instant responses to some of these games. A few have been revised - and you have the polished articles, gifts from them to you. There are flash length pieces, complete short stories, a play, poems, all sorts. So, you can see for yourself the endless possibilities open to us in interpreting these stimuli. They aren't there to copy, or emulate, and aren't intended to be the best of anything, just examples, offered by other writers. I have picked them though, for that indefinable something - a creative spark. We all hope you enjoy them. I hope that seeing how others have interpreted the exercises will underline how unique we all are. How often have I heard, "I've never written like that before!" from a writer who is gazing at their page of scribble after a ten-minute game, a glazed look on their face. To which the only answer has to be, "No? Why Not? You have now." There is richness below the surface of all of us. But we can all get stuck in ruts, and sometimes it takes a game to break us out of that pattern.

Please believe in your creative uniqueness. Only you see the world as you do, and only you can write like you. Whether you choose to dive into the cold water and swim, whether you choose to work with an existing character or project – it doesn't matter. Have at it!

Let's play.

Vanessa

GAMES 1 TO 10 - WORD CRICKET

I've been told that I invented this game, but I'm not sure about that. It is so simple, and so effective – over the last decade or so, I've heard of it being played all over the place. Really, it doesn't matter who invented it. I'm sure there are a hundred versions out there. This is mine.

Word Cricket is simply magic for helping the writer to relax and go with the flow. It can help to dispel those worries we all have about not being 'good enough'. And fear of that blank page. Writer's block... whatever you call it. Remember – no one is going to see what you write unless you choose to share it.

Find a quiet corner when you have 20 minutes to yourself, sit back, relax, and have a go.

In cricket, you catch a ball (or try to!) if you are fielding. Here, you catch words as you are writing. If you are writing alone, scribble words on slips of paper, screw them up, stick them in a mug, and, starting with the opening phrase I give you, write for a minute or two, (set a timer if you want) then take out a word at random. I suggest you don't cheat and put it back for a 'better' word. There isn't one. The only rule is, make it fit in the sentence you are writing, or the next one. Or maybe the one after that – but incorporate it, fast.

Flex the word to fit, if you like, but it must fit the flow of words you have started. Thus, 'change' could be a verb, or a noun. It could be a changing room, or a changing mat. It could become a changeling, or the weather could be changeable. Your character could run out of change, or the traffic lights might change. There are endless possibilities! (I said 'flow of words' rather than 'story' because it might be something else. Don't judge yourself - you are writing a 'thing' and that's cool.)

Set the timer again, continue with the piece you've started. When the timer goes off, take the next word, and make it fit.

You can see when the word pile is half done, and when you only have a few left, then two then one…

Keep going. By this point, you might well have a decent starter – characters, something happening, something to resolve.

In the next few pages, you have ten starter phrases and word lists to play with. And plenty of room to add your own lists, or ask other writers to gift you lists. White space is to be written on.

In Part Two, I also give you a few examples other writers have come up with. Have fun!

CRICKET 1

On the calendar, the next day didn't exist…

Enemy

Curlew

Hotel

Fog

Geometry

Seed

Cushion

Hell

Migraine

Science

CRICKET 2

I couldn't stand her…

Persimmon

Pineapple

Permeate

Presence

Pride

Plumbline

Patient

Pristine

Pants

Penny

CRICKET 3

She stopped the car and turned around…

Tinnitus

Darkness

Acid

Scuttle

Mother

Ammonia

Reflection

Monochrome

Blade

Pyjamas

CRICKET 4

On my doorstep, a package. On the package, no name…

Purple

Johannesburg

Ice cream

Ammonia

Ants

Shiver

Bell

History

Stick

Morning

CRICKET 5

I've always hated flying…

Poppy

Albatross

Kindly

Bigamy

Fortune

Stable

Cairo

Coward

Coaldust

Unforgettable

CRICKET 6

Let's change the tempo. Now, you're going to pay Word Cricket with one of your characters. This is great for surprising yourself, for letting your characters speak for themselves, not controlling them too much. You need to be really aware when you are stepping in and answering what *you* want the word to be, rather than your character.

For that reason, some of the prompt words are generic – a place, a number, a colour, a discovery – something they, not you, add and run with. If you possibly can, feel that difference?

Same rules: a half starter that your character runs with. Not you. Then ten prompts to incorporate every minute or so. Let your characters surprise you!

Last night I dreamed...

A scent

Darkness

A colour

A number

A food

Pain

A place

A parent

A discovery

Ladder

CRICKET 7

We ran with a Burns Night special on a Grist to the Mill creative workshop, with some lovely results. So here it is:

Your title: Ode to a Haggis - and just write!

Thrissle

Brattle

Wanton

Sonsie

Slickit

Bonnie

Ferlie

Giftie

Blethering

Bethankit

CRICKET 8 - the key to difficult stories.

I have used Word Cricket in various guises, to help me unlock a piece of work I'm finding difficult. Initially, working with a tutor who used to feed us lists of words, I was very stuck with a short story that was digging at very personal stuff. I was getting close to the end, but I was uncomfortable, so I put it away and didn't continue. Then, over a year later, after playing with loads of these lists and writing other stories, a list appeared, headed by two words. Green balloon. I was instantly back to my lost story. I found it, took a deep breath, and continued where I'd left off. It was still difficult, but the words helped me to unpick the lock.

Those words are all still there, towards the end of the short story that became the title story of my first collection, *Words from a Glass Bubble (Salt Publishing)*. So, here is the same list.

You can try it with a piece of work you are stuck with – not necessarily this list – as the words might seriously not fit what you were writing, and that's fine. Look at the other lists. Maybe you can use one of those in the same way? Try one at random? Ask someone else to supply the list?

Maybe write a fresh story?

Green balloon

Concrete

Pigeon

Xylophone

Plastic

Bean stick

Hip

Mask

Malta

Whisper

CRICKET 9

They were walking straight towards me, carrying….

Ink

Passion

Screwdriver

Violence

Chocolate

Feathers

Marble

Toenail

Sinful

Spain

CRICKET 10

Let's finish with another change of tempo. If you are working on something, use these to open up the next scenes.

Or, start a new short story with these, or, as writer Sylvia Petter did in a workshop, start a novel - (the opening is in Part Two)

In the middle of the city...

Thief

Partridge

Mirror

Honeybee

Prison

Motorbike

Manipulate

Brass

Brothers

Ticket

What's the secret to Word Cricket lists?

I'm often asked what the secret is – it must be in the word lists?

Not at all. There is no secret. If you want to share this with your writer's group, here you go – this is what I do. I might pick up a book and take four or five nouns at random, things that seem not to go together. That seem interesting.

I choose one or two words that open up an emotional possibility – one or two with scents associated with them, or sounds, or textures. I might chuck in a random place name. A food. A make of car. The name of a mountain, a country. Getting the idea? Anything!

Starter phrases need to make good jump-off points without saying too much. 'She stopped the car and turned around' could be any scenario from a shopping trip to a kidnap, to a holiday gone wrong, to a … well, you tell me.

In your writing group (the preamble 'instructions' are at the start of this chapter), try to write quickly and not plan, and incorporate each word as it drops into the air.

It's a good idea to say if anyone doesn't know the word, or doesn't hear it, use what they think they heard, or make it up. No one's checking.

Get them going and let them write quickly for a minute or two. Prompt them to write faster if it looks like some are over-thinking. When everyone's settled, chuck in the first word. And again, every minute or so.

I usually say when I am halfway through the list, and when there are three, two and one word left. When the list is exhausted, the writers won't be, so let them carry on for as long as you like.

Enjoy! It's a good ice breaker.

GAME 11 - THINKING SIDEWAYS or Don't just mention the egg cup. Throw it at someone.

This is a variation on the 'list' idea, but with all the words (or items) in front of you. And you have two things to do, in two separate games.

First, incorporate them all into a story/flash/poem/thing.

Second, make them shape-shift. What I mean is, each item can only be added if it has a reason to be within the piece. So, don't just mention the egg cup: use it.

Here's your list of Things:

Egg cup

Candlestick

Postcard

Honesty

Berlin

Ginger

Holly

Laptop

Vinegar

Crossword

Remember, when each Thing is mentioned, something must happen. Don't just mention the egg cup. Throw it at someone. (Metaphorically…)

Or

When is an egg cup not just an egg cup?

When I say something has to happen, be careful. I don't mean momentous things. It might be tiny – something internal to the character who is noticing the egg cup. If they are noticing it. Why are they noticing it? What's in their heads? If it's the narrator noticing it – why? What is the thing in the story for? Think sideways, and your character, or your narrator will.

Eg, one of these?:

Turn that upside down, it'd make a great finial.

That's it. Boiled eggs for tea.

Hang on – there were two there this morning. Where's the other one?

Egg cup? Not mine. Where did that come from?

God's sake, George, haven't we got proper salt? The Vicar's coming for lunch.

Honestly officer, when I threw the egg cup at his head, I never realised it was made of lead.

Tip: read the word list. And this works with all these list games. Spend a little time just looking and contemplating, before jumping. *Feel* which words or objects you are drawn to or repulsed by, if any - there are arguments that suggest the latter might be the best inspiration… and the only instruction is no to:
On the table happened to be an egg cup, a candlestick, a book of crosswords, a postcard, a guidebook of Berlin, a bit of ginger and a bottle of vinegar.

An egg cup can't just be on the table en passant. Something has to happen with each thing you use. The story must shift a little. And you have to use them all.

See Part Two for an example of how a writer used this game to think sideways and kick start a series of short stories.

GAME 12 – USING IMAGES (i) BOY ON THE BEACH

Choose somewhere quiet, where you know you won't be disturbed, and set aside at least half an hour.

When you are settled, look at the image for what seems a long while – three or four minutes. Longer if you want to. Really *see* everything. Let the image speak to your creative spirit.

Take notes if that works for you. Make a word cloud.

And respond in words. The words might come slowly, and that's fine. Just write down what rises up. If you prefer, write down what you see – literally

– then explore what cues you pick up from the boy. And trust that as you write, more will come up to join those first words. Keep going, even if it feels sticky.

Please don't edit as you go. Let the words flow without censoring them. Spelling mistake? So what? Half a sentence?

Keep going!

It really, seriously doesn't matter what you write. It might start as one thing then veer off to become something else. It might be a short story. It might be a poem. It might evoke a memory, then veer off to somewhere else. It might be a mix of everything.

I'd like you to write for at least twenty minutes, and longer if the piece takes off.

There are no rights and wrongs. Like everything else in this book, this helps you create a draft. It does not have to be perfect.

There are some lovely responses to this image at the back of the book.

GAME 13 – USING IMAGES (ii)

STAIRCASE TO NOWHERE - Find your own picture

Use Shutterstock or another photo archive and search 'staircase to nowhere'. There are brilliant places to find brilliant inspirational images. Some are royalty-free, most aren't. Find a photo that speaks to you, on your screen.

And the advice is the same as before. To recap:

Your instructions are very simple. Be somewhere quiet, where you know you won't be disturbed, and set aside at least half an hour.

When you are settled, look at the image of the staircase to nowhere. Notice all the changes in texture in those bricks. What are they trying to say? That shadow? That window?

Take notes if that works for you and respond in words. Explore what cues you pick up.

GAME 14 - MUSIC AND WRITING

You're going to write to *Spiegl im Spiegl*, by Arvo Part. It is the most dreamlike and relaxing piece, which makes a perfect non-intrusive background to writing. And a wonderfully relaxing half hour if you decide to just listen.

There is a particularly good version on YouTube in which Renaud Capuçon plays the violin with pianist Guillaume Bellom. Or you might have access to this piece another way. The piece lasts about ten minutes. If you can put it on a loop, so much the better.

Sit quietly in the music for a while. Let it work on you, making you relax. And notice your breath slowing.

You can either start writing whatever comes, and enjoy that,

or better…

Try this. You need a little time, an hour, perhaps, and the space should be just yours.

Sink into these. You are aiming at ten minutes per prompt:

Beauty

Water

Grief

Loneliness

Peace

Light

Pick these in order and write to the music. For a few minutes, as you listen and float, jot down words that seem to attach themselves to the sounds. Make a sound-word cloud, thinking and listening. Don't censor yourself if a word comes into your head that you feel you shouldn't or mustn't write about. Why not? Who's watching?

When you have your cloud, write for five minutes or more, using your words as hooks for the prose. Or use the words to write a poem. If a narrative emerges, stick with that, and carry on for the remainder of the piece. If you get stuck, stop, sit back, and just enjoy the moment.

Start the music again. This time, write to 'water'. Same 'rules'.

Then write to 'grief'. Look after yourself – you may not want to write to this one - and that's fine.

And so on – until each ten minutes is up, the mood changes, the emotion shifts, and perhaps one will merge with the next, as the poetry, story or 'thing' shifts.

I suggest you keep these prompt words in order, so you return to 'Peace' and 'Light' at the end? Start positive, drop into contemplative, return to the light.

I ought to add, other composers work, too, but not as well as Arvo Part. Bach, Mozart – they work too, but some pieces are better than others. There is also a two-hour long compilation of classics for writing, from Halidon Music. Try it out on Youtube.

One writer who has kindly sent me some lovely work for Part Two, Maria Sanger, says this: "*The choice of Arvo Part was very effective because of the 'sleep walking' nature, whereas I had perhaps consciously chosen classical pieces I liked in the past, but which were possibly too active for the purposes of writing a poem.*"

GAME 15 – INSPIRATION FROM BOOKS

THE LOST PIANOS OF SIBERIA by SOPHY ROBERTS

We all find inspiration when we read, but some books are better than others. If you find one that works for you, don't give it away!

The Lost Pianos of Siberia is, for me, such a book.

In one chapter, we meet a local character who is known in his community as The Minister for Bizarre Affairs.

Your job is to recruit for such a job. Write a job description for The Minister of Bizarre Affairs that will include the overall responsibilities, the people reporting to them, the types of things they will be expected to do to fulfil this role.

And then, a Person Specification. Imagine you are recruiting for such a minister for the government of a country. What sort of person would fill the job you have just described?

Is there a story here?

GAME 16 – THE PIANO TUNER AT THE END OF THE WORLD

An idea, a character to create, a scenario to explore:

Google the city of Ushuaia, in Tierra del Fuego.

It really is getting close to the ends of the earth. Cruise ships start their journeys to Antarctica from here. Find out about the history of the place. The loneliness. Such that for decades the main reason for Ushuaia was its prison. A desolate place indeed.

Now consider this scenario: Two ships have docked, and the passengers have disembarked. The ships are being prepared for their next trip, leaving later today or tomorrow. A man is walking down to the ships carrying a small case, too small for the man to be a passenger, and he doesn't look prepared for a journey.

He's a piano tuner, on his way to check over the pianos on both these ships. A few weeks in the cold air, the constantly changing levels of humidity caused by the doors opening and closing on the inflatables that take the passengers to land, and their need for warmth when back on board, takes its toll on the two instruments.

People say he's lived here for over twenty years. And he is skilled, top of his profession.

Your challenge:

Who is he?

Why has he chosen to work here of all places?

What happened to bring him to this place, of all the cities in the world where he could have chosen to work?

Imagine: one day, he falls asleep beneath a piano in a small ship's lounge and only wakes when the ship starts to move…

GAME 17 – MISSING PERSONS / WANTED PERSONS

Plan out a missing person poster. Include when the person was last seen and where. Be concise. It will mainly be a space for an image of the person's face and a few words.

or

A wanted poster - including what the person has done to be wanted by the authorities. Again, be concise with the words.

Now, add in YOUR face. You are that missing or wanted person.

You can do many different things with this one. Here are some suggestions:

Why are 'you' missing? Write a first-person narrative as the missing person… whatever's happened?

Why are 'you' wanted? What have you done? Did you do it, or is it a case of mistaken identity? What can you do now? How do you get out of this one?

Or

You (or your character) see the missing person, or the wanted person going into a train station. What happens? Quick!

Have fun!

GAME 18 – BATH TIME

This game comes from writer, editor and teacher Zoe King, who used this as part of a visualisation exercise for writers. I won't do the visualisation bit, but here's your scenario:

You (or your character, of course) have had a warm bath, and when you get out you reach for the cosy dressing gown that's hanging behind the door. But instead of a dressing gown, there's someone or something else's skin hanging in its place. It doesn't feel strange at all. It feels safe and intriguing. You can slip out of your own skin and put on this, and when you want to, you can put yours back on.

What was hanging there when you first read this strange little prompt? Whatever it was, try to go back to that and go on – put it on, and write what happens.

It doesn't have to be human, does it? It could be anything! I've shared this one with school students and they've had great fun becoming sharks, wasps, and dinosaurs. If it is human, it doesn't have to be contemporary. What about a fictional character?

Anything or anyone!

GAME 19 – USING REAL LIFE STORIES AS INSPIRATION

There's Someone in My House!

On The Guardian online, dated 10th September 2021, find the article entitled, 'Experience: A Stranger Secretly Lived in my Home.'

After reading the first few paragraphs, write around this strange scenario, asking yourself questions:

What do you need to know?

Who is hiding?

Where are they hiding?

How long have they been there?

Why are they there?

When are they found?

How are they found? or.... Are they?

You can do this in several ways:

Use first person to write a narrative from the point of view of the person whose home it is.

Another first-person piece, and a narrative from the point of view of the intruder.

A police report.

A journalistic article.

Looking back or forwards twenty-five years later.

Or think of your own way to approach the scenario.

GAME 20 - THE VISITORS' BOOK

You are checking in at a hotel for the night, on your own. You've never been here before. At reception, they ask you to sign the visitor book and add your address, and your car registration.

Opening the book, it falls open at a page from two years ago where you see your own name at the top of the page. The same car registration. Your address. But you've definitely never been here before...

Keep going...

Try first person...

Try third person...

Try it from the receptionist's point of view...

Try second person...

GAME 21 - BEAUTIFUL WORDS / UGLY WORDS

This comes with thanks to the late Karen Blomain, novelist, poet, teacher. Karen was a generous, supportive and absolutely lovely person. She was known for her poetry, her novels, her essays and stage work. Sadly, she died in 2012. But I know how terrific this idea was for me, as the piece of writing I did in response, amazingly, and tidied of course, went on to win a small short story competition, and be broadcast on local radio (BBC Southern Counties/Guildford Book Festival, 2006). I put that early success down to having no pressure at all to write.

The group word list we ended up with that day was as follows:

Ugly words:

Clog

Euthanasia

Parsimonious

Holocaust

Gusset

Beautiful words:

Gunnera

Phalaenopsis

Flawless

Epiphany

Lilac

You could do this with a writing group or on your own.

In a group, ask everyone to think of a word they find ugly and one they find beautiful. If doing it on your own, think up perhaps six 'ugly' words and six 'beautiful' words. Collate them into a list, and in no more than 20 minutes, incorporate them all into one story draft.

The story I came up with, *Naming Finbar*, is in a short story collection called *A Short History of Synchronised Breathing* (Cultured Llama).

GAME 22 – THE PRAM

Some lovely creepy stories can come from this one.

You are walking along a path and see a woman walking towards you, pushing a pram. For some reason, you don't quite trust her.

How is she walking?

How does she look at you as she gets closer? Or does she?

What about the pram? What is it like? You can tell the reader a lot about characters by describing not her, but something that belongs to her.

What is she doing?

You have to step off the path to let the woman past. She doesn't react. No thanks, no eye-contact.

As she passes you, you peek into the pram to see the baby.

But it isn't a baby.

EEK.

What's in the pram?!

What happens?

GAME 23 – INSPIRATION FROM POETRY

Poetry provides the writer in me with more inspirations than any other medium. It is a powerful respource. Usually, it is the rhythms, the sounds that open up rivers of words. Sometimes, it is collisions of images. Sometimes, a poem will spark an idea, for me to explore.

Here, in a game I first met in a workshop led by Dean Atta, you riff off an existing poem - but I have found that the memories that drive the new piece spark further ideas - it's like chucking a coin in to a still pond.

Google "I COME FROM" poems. You'll find some humdingers online, including good ones by Dean Atta himself, Sydney Morris, Robert Seatter, and others.

Either write your own.

or

Ask your character to write one. Who knows, you might find out a lot about them that you didn't know before.

GAME 24 – TWO STRANGERS ON A TRAIN

You need to have two characters with very little in common. Think of anyone you like, as far apart as you can. On one occasion, playing this game, a writer decided to work with Anne Boleyn (the real one) and a young black teenager. See what I mean?!

Your job is to get them to stand next to each other on a train platform, waiting for the same train. (Yes, Anne Boleyn too…)

The train arrives, they go to get on, but both want to get on first.

There is an altercation.

They then find they have to sit together.

And all kinds ensue.

Write that scene, just using dialogue. You need to remember how differently people speak, their different values, different everything!

Have fun.

PS. The writer who worked with Anne Boleyn and the black teenager continued with her scene and submitted it to a playwriting competition for unpublished writers. It had its first showing at Camden Peoples' Theatre in March 2023.

GAME 25 – RANDOM NUMBERS

Choose a three-digit number – anything you like. Google it… and follow your nose as you discover random facts linked to your number.

Eg

I google 479 as I'm writing this, so what you are getting below is happening in 'real time'. I've discovered the following:

1. 479 is the number of the bus from Guildford to Epsom via Leatherhead
2. 479 is the area code for thirteen counties in the northwestern area of the US state of Arkansas, including the cities of Bentonville, Fort Smith, Fayetteville, Rogers, Siloam Springs, and Springdale.
3. 479 was a common year starting on Monday of the Julian Calendar. There's a list of historical events, births and deaths that occurred during this year.
4. The Victoria towel rail/radiator, supplied by Phoenix, is 952mm X 479mm.
5. The Emily Dickinson poem, 'Because I could not stop for Death' is 479th on the Poetry Foundation's website.
6. A watercolour paint advertised on the SAA artists' website is: Schmincke Horad Artists' Watercolours - Helio Cerulean - Half Pan - (Series 1) (479)
7. On Experian, a credit score of 479 is below the average credit score. Many lenders choose not to do business with borrowers whose scores fall in the Very Poor area.
8. SikaForce-479 L45 is a two-component polyurethane adhesive which cures by chemical reaction.

(Tip: They get more interesting the further you go. Use as many as you like to create a story. The more unlikely the collisions, the better.)

GAME 26 – RANDOM DATES

As before, only Google random dates.

Again, in real-time as I'm writing this, I googled May 5th, 1905, and discovered the following facts. It's the date on which the following happened:

1. Robert S Abbott published 1st issue of newspaper *Chicago Defender.*
2. Arnold Meijer, Dutch leader of the fascist Dutch National & Black Front, was born in Haarlemmermeer, Netherlands.
3. Floyd Gottfredson, American cartoonist, was born – primarily known for the *Mickey Mouse* comic strip; born in Kaysville, Utah.
4. Korea University was founded in Seoul.
5. The calendar for the year 2023 is the same as that for 1905.
6. There's a whole mass of information in The New York Times for this date. Articles include 'Aunt held as Kidnapper' and 'Englishman and his American Wife could not agree so decided to die together'.

You can either collide these disparate discoveries or pick one and run with that. Whatever you do, it will be interesting.

GAME 27 – TURNING THINGS ON THEIR HEADS

Thanks to writer, editor and teacher Tania Hershman for inspiring this one.

This is a simple game, but with anything but simple outcomes.

Take any short draft, and run it backwards, sentence by sentence, adjust the syntax so it makes sense, and stand back. Read it through.

How has the piece shifted?

Has anything new come into focus?

Try turning it into a mirror. Tidy the original piece and leave an empty line, then add the 'new' backwards version at the bottom, so it starts and ends with almost exactly the same sentence.

Is it 'better' moving forwards, moving backwards, or mirrored?

If you shift the separate sentences around, can you make something different again?

Why not? Who's watching?

GAME 28 – CHANNELLING KAFKA

In The Metamorphosis, Franz Kafka invents a character, Gregor Samsa, who wakes up one ordinary morning, changed into an insect. The voice of the whole narrative is dead pan, accepting that this has happened. Here is that opening:

The Metamorphosis, *translated by Andrew Wylie.*

One morning, when Gregor Samsa woke from troubled dreams, he found himself transformed in his bed into horrible vermin. He lay on his armour-like back, and if he lifted his head a little, he could see his brown belly, slightly domed and divided by arches into stiff sections. The bedding was hardly able to cover it and seemed ready to slide off any moment. His many legs, pitifully thin compared with the size of the rest of him, waved about helplessly as he looked.

"What's happened to me?" he thought. It wasn't a dream. His room, a proper human room although a little too small, lay peacefully between its four familiar walls. A collection of textile samples lay spread out on the table—Samsa was a travelling salesman—

Gregor is quite ordinary and yet this extraordinary thing has happened to him. The novel unfolds as he works out how to live like this.

Your task is to use the same event, a character waking up on an ordinary day, but waking as something different, or indeed someone different.

Or: Be a creature you wouldn't want to be, in a place you love - or the other way round.

Try it in the first person.

In the third person, like Kafka.

In the second person… see how it shifts in each different perspective.

Which perspective is the most successful? Which does the story want to be told in?

GAME 29 – N+7

This is one of my favourite games, invented by the Oulipo* group of writers. See more about them below… a fascinating bunch. Thanks to David Gaffney for introducing me to this lot.

Here, you can take any piece of writing – a whole flash, a micro – and you need to be armed with a dictionary. All you do is take each noun, find it in your dictionary, count seven words on in the dictionary and substitute it for your original noun.

Sounds nuts? Yep – but can have strangely logical outcomes, and at the very least, can send your piece of work to other realms. It's a bit of fun… and I'll never stop saying it – we need to play!

Here's an example of one paragraph of a commission I'm working on, so you can see how it works. It can sometimes stop you being quite so serious. Here's the serious version:

I fetched my glasses. Of course, there was no one outside and that brought a sudden emptiness into the pit of my stomach.

I was telling myself off for being fanciful, and I saw it again – a low flight from one tree to another, closer to the window. Like a shadow. A bird. A sparrowhawk. Of course, we see them in the orchard, coming out of the woods, going after the smaller birds – the goldfinches, the linnets, and the sparrows of course – but I have not seen one perch up before. I haven't known one choose a tree quite so in the open, and quite so close to a house.

This becomes the gloriously nutty:

I fetched my gleams. Of course, there was no one outside and that brought a sudden emulsion into the pitchfork of my stonecrop.

I was telling myself off for being fanciful, and I saw it again – a low flint from one tremble to another, closer to the windsurfer. Like a shake. A birthday. A spat. Of course, we see them in the orderly, come out of the woollens, going after the smaller birthdays – the Goliaths, the lints, and the spats of course – but I have not seen one perch up before. I haven't known one choose a tremble quite so in the opera, and quite so close to a housekeeper.

Well, that final sentence, about choosing trembles at operas, close to housekeepers, could well spark something fun if I'm in the right mood. A new story from a pile of er… is it rubbish? Nah. See what I mean?! Go for it.

(Also try N + any other number you like. Your text will shift gloriously from one thing to another as you play.)

* OULIPO (from Wikipedia)

A loose gathering of (mainly) French-speaking writers and mathematicians who seek to create works using constrained writing techniques. It was founded in 1960.

The group defines the term littérature potentielle as (rough translation): "the seeking of new structures and patterns which may be used by writers in any way they enjoy". Queneau described Oulipians as "rats who construct the labyrinth from which they plan to escape."

Constraints are used as a means of triggering ideas and inspiration.

GAME 30 – MESSAGE IN A BOTTLE

Use your mate Google to find an image of an old bottle. Whichever seems most interesting to you. Whichever seems to contain something to say.

There's a really good one on the BBC News website from 19 November 2022 under the heading, "135-year-old message in a bottle found under floorboards".

Quietly sit and look at the bottle and make notes for a good five minutes. Every detail. What does it make you think of? What are the connections? What links do those connections connect to? Spin it into a spidergram. Let your mind wander.

And then, imagine someone finds this bottle – but where? Make notes.

And when?

Something is inside. A piece of paper, brown with age. Describe what you see.

How do you get it out without it falling to dust?

What does it say?

And then…?

Always keep an eye on the News. Pick out quirky stories which might lead somewhere. There are a few good ones scattered through this book, but you can find your own, every day. Unexpected stories, unexpected poetry. It's such a great exercise to strengthen that story-finding muscle.

From the BBC News story referenced above:

A plumber could not believe his eyes when he cut a hole in floorboards in an Edinburgh house and found a bottle containing a 135-year-old message.

Peter Allan, 50, discovered the Victorian time capsule when he opened up the floor in the exact spot where the whisky bottle had been left.

PS: In this case: *The note was signed and dated by two male workers and read: "James Ritchie and John Grieve laid this floor, but they did not drink the whisky. October 6th, 1887. Whoever finds this bottle may think our dust is blowing along the road."*

Isn't that beautiful? James Ritchie and John Grieve were philosopher-poets as well as whatever else they did. Imagine what questions flow from that for a writer.

GAME 31 – WRITING TO SCENTS/ SMELLS

SMELL THE COFFEE

For this, you will need a cup of coffee, a spoon of instant coffee, or a jar of freshly ground coffee.

To begin, all you need to do is smell the coffee. As always, take your time.

Where does the smell take you? Make notes. What places? What company are you in? What memories rise up?

As words rise up, write them down, even those you aren't sure of, or 'don't want to write.'

Make a word cloud.

Either:

1. Use this word cloud to create a 'thing'

2. Use the cloud to write a narrative

3. A poem

or

Find two characters and write a short scene of dialogue, which is triggered by one of your words.

Or see if they will be sparked by both the smell of coffee and these words:

Jealousy

Laughter

Fire

Flying

You can replicate this game many times, using all kinds of scents – spices work particularly well. You could also use perfumes, especially old ones – lavender, perhaps, or violet – see where they take you.

GAME 32 - WEIRD OCCUPATIONS!

(with apologies to anyone who works as a professional snuggler…)

Check out websites that list weird occupations. Find ones that spark you, make you think, or make you go 'wow!', 'yuk!' or any other reaction. You are listening/feeling for a reaction.

Here's a selection from one website – these are apparently current occupations, real live things one can do, and obviously some people do – but what a wonderful thing for inventing characters?!

Professional bridesmaid
Professional mourner
Snake milker
Professional snuggler
Movie watcher
Iceberg mover
Professional foreigner
Professional queuer
Human statue
Soap boiler
Dog food tester/ pet food taster
Online dating ghostwriter
etc etc.

Here's a list of historic strange occupations, which could take you into a historic narrative:

Leech collector
Knocker-up
Lector
Ice cutter
Daguerrotypist
Groom of the stool

or

Google strange job titles listed on old censuses, perhaps.

This is how respondents described themselves in the 1881 census. Many of them make me feel sad, make me want to know who they were, what happened to them. Writing is a lovely way of bringing part of them back. I've used this list many times. Try it?

52 Years an Imbecile
Artificial Scone Maker
Assisting at Mangle
Beef Twister
Bottle Washer
Bounder
Boy for General Purposes
Carrot and Mangle Salesman
Cleans Onions
Clod Hopper (FT) *(as opposed to part time?! VG)*
Colourist of Artificial Fish
Count as Female
Cow Banger (Ag Lab)
Curer of Smokey Chimneys
Custard Maker (Carpet)
Dead
Decayed Publisher (No Occ) *(I suspect some of these comments are by the official filler in of forms. Now there's another possiblity. VG)*
Describes Himself as Leaving No Trace
Disinfector of Railway (Oths)
Dog Performer
Driving Channel Tunnel
Drowner
Egg Breaker
Egg Cracker
Electric Bath Attendant
Emasculator
Employed with Head Off
Examiner of Underclothing
Fatuous Pauper

Feeder in Bump Factory
Feeding Boy to Printing Machine
Ferret Weaver
Fish Bender
Floater
Follows Wifely Occupations
Formerly Fat
Gold Fish Catcher
Grape Dryer
Gymnast to House Painter
Hand in Hartleys Jam
Head of Female
He Play All Day Long
Invalid Kings Evil
Invisible Net Maker
Keeps Own House at Home
Knight of the Thimble
Knocker Up of Workpeople
Maker of Sand Views
Pensioner in Charge of the Magnet
Prime Minister (No Occ)
Proprietor of Midgets
Proprietor of Solution For Protection of Turnip From Fly
Random Waller
Ripper Coalmine (Blows Roof Down)
Rotters Boy
Running About
Runs Abt Selling Fish (Hawker)
Rust Attendant at a Lavatory
Sampler of Drugs
Scarecrow
Seperated from Head
Sick Maker
Slob Brickmaker
Supposed to be a Lady
Teacher of Wax Flowers

Tender of Charge of Cubes
Tool Maker (Screws) Wife *(Oh for a little posessive apostrophe and s! VG)*
Travels With an Entire Horse
Turnip Shepherd
Unsettled Through Recent Death
Very Feeble
Watchmaker Master (No Hands)

If you can't find something here, then um, try again after a glass of wine?

I'm the sort of writer who will just jump in and write to find out who and why this might be, but you might prefer to work with some queries first, to open out the background narrative:

Who is doing this thing?

How did they fall into it?

Why are they doing it?

What is it giving them that more regular occupations don't/can't/wouldn't? (Actually, what's regular, anyway?).

GAME 33 – OCCUPATIONS AND ACTIVITIES

From the previous game, you have a load of occupations, either modern or historical. You can add, for this one, a list of ordinary occupations, if you like. Come up with your own list of ten that interest you or worry you – but definitely not ones that make you think 'meh'.

Now, pair up those occupations with the following list of activities:

Picking all the blue flowers in the park

Painting over the insides of the windows

Burying silver spoons in the garden

Dismantling a motorbike and hiding the parts

Tearing out the final page of the book

Buying a one-way ticket to the last town on the island

Breaking into a house to put things back

Walking in an absolutely straight line through the village. (Think about it, it can be done but not easily – your character has to walk through houses, over walls, through streams…)

Writing a letter to someone they've never met

Now, your job is to pick one pair and write a flash/short story/something – you'll find an example in Part Two. Ask yourself, why is my character doing this? What's happened?

Going forward, this one is easy to put together and share. You just need an eye for strangeness, in both occupations and possibly odd activities – things that don't seem to go together. Make up your own lists.

You can, working with your writing group, write each occupation and activity on slips of paper, and let each writer pick one from each set at random. It's a great game to warm up a writing session.

GAME 34 – MEMORY LOOP

1. Choose one memory and write it down – something you like, because the scenario is that all your other memories will be wiped. This one is the only one you are allowed to have, and it will be played on a loop.

2. Change one thing in the first sentence and see how that change flows out into the whole piece.

3. Change another thing in that new first sentence, and let it flow through the piece…

Keep going until the memory is completely different.

Or

Take a tip from Game 27 and run it backwards… see what happens!

Maybe reshape them into a series of interlinked short somethings.

GAME 35 – MEMORY LOOP OULIPO GAME

From the last game:

1. Take your original memory as you wrote it, and rewrite it, this time omitting any word containing the letter 'i'. It means finding another way to say whatever that word was doing. You might need to rephrase that whole sentence, or only change it slightly.

2. Take that new 'i'-free memory, and rewrite it, this time omitting the letter 'e'. You are changing this second version, remember? As before, you will no doubt need to rethink the way you said certain things, to say something similar with no 'e'! (But you can have your 'i' back…)

3. Meld the two versions to make a third piece.

4. Keep playing, watch it change. Rewrite with no 'o'?

Compare:

The original memory

One related with no Os

One related with no Es

One related with no Is.

The melded versions

How have they changed? Do they make a pattern, a new 'something'?

PS – You can play this game with any piece of writing, of course. Have at it!

GAME 36 – TINS

Imagine a cupboard filled with tinned food, but all the labels have gone.

You can take two tins. You're with someone else. Who? Where are you? When are you? Why are you eating from tins and why only two?

Choose two, and make a meal for something or someone…

Or

Writing in the first person, you are the one taking labels off in someone else's house. Why? What are you trying to achieve? What did they do?

Or

Starting with these tins in the cupboard, in a house you have just entered, describe the kitchen and the rest of the house. If those tins are blank, what is the rest of the house like?

Check out Part Two for an example story in response.

GAME 37 - INSPIRATION FROM SHORT STORIES

RILKE - *THE WRECKED HOUSES, THE BIG THING*

I came across this terrific story in *Randall Jarrell's Book of Stories**, which, if you are interested in short fiction, is a must. It was recommended by George Saunders, both for the stories, and for Jarrell's superb introductory essay on the short story in general.

One story therein is by Rainer Rilke, and this story contains the most compelling description of a house of which the front wall has collapsed.

This is part of the description:

The most unforgettable of all were the walls themselves. The stubborn life of these rooms had not let itself be trampled out. It was still there; it clung to the nails that had been left, it stood on the remaining handsbreadth of flooring, it crouched under the corner joints where there was still a little bit of interior. One could see that it was the paint, which, year by year, it had slowly altered: blue into moldy green, green into grey, and yellow into an old, stale rotting white. But it was also in the spots that had kept fresher, behind mirrors, pictures and wardrobes.

From The Wrecked House, by Rainer Maria Rilke

So – off we go. I'd like you to take time over this, slowly imagining you are standing in front of a wrecked residential building - think Blitz, earthquake, missiles - and gradually build up a picture of the lives that were lived here, now shattered, from the details that come to you, things you can see in each of the now ruined, open-fronted rooms.

Is there a story here, long or short? One writer sent me a piece that came out of this idea, the longest short story she had written in a long while. Part of that story, and her own description of how it worked for her, is in Part Two.

* *Randall Jarrell's Book of Stories* is referenced in the Resources section at the end of this book.

GAME 38 – LOST PROPERTY (1)

Google The New Yorker, September 10th 2017, and find an article about an office for Lost and Found articles in Paris, entitled The Peculiar Poetry of Paris's Lost and Found.

The Bureau of Found Objects is over 200 years old and still receives 600-700 items daily; items left on the Metro, at stations, airports, or found in the street, etc.

Who knew? But this is a treasure box! Even if you are unable to access the website, the salient points are right here.

You can read about Veronique Balsam who was aged 21 when she went in to take dictation for some letters. Thirty-five years later, in 2017, she was still there…

Here are just some of the items lost and handed in – behind each one, there is a story, or many stories… surely. Take a look and pick whichever one jumps out at you today. Write about it. Bring it to life. Whose is it? Who lost it, and how? Why? Where? And what are they doing without it? How is its absence eating at them?

Pouch of diamonds

Gas mask

Unworn wedding dress and shoes

Replica streetlamp

Medals

Military uniforms

Sabre

Human skull

Three pieces of concrete from the World Trade Center

A stuffed lobster

A collection of blue butterflies…

GAME 39 – NEWTS IN THE KITCHEN

(with enormous thanks to Electra Rhodes)

I read a wonderful tweet by the brilliant writer Electra Rhodes. It fizzed with fun, energy, playfulness and a sprinkling of magic, so I asked her permission to use it as inspiration in workshops – and to reprint it here. Lucky us. Here it is:

Ages ago, I rented a house that had newts living in the half-basement kitchen when I moved in. I also found a small cauldron, a tiny leather suitcase and the ingredients and recipes for dreams, weather, and revolutions. The newts were successfully relocated. The rest I kept, in case.

So, why not move in somewhere, find something already there, something a little bit strange and magical. Here, part of the piece's success, for me, is that list:

'Dreams, weather and revolutions…'

What do your magical ingredients do? Good things, benign interesting things, or not so good?

Such responsibility!

GAME 40 – BEGINNINGS, WITH A BLANK SCREEN

Find any short story anthology on your shelves and flip through to the opening lines. Pick ones you like and use them as springboards.

Set a timer for 20 minutes, then jump off your chosen board and swim like crazy. Only here, just for fun, you are going to cover the screen, or type white on white, so you can't see what you are doing – and just go for it. Run!

When the timer goes, stop. Uncover the screen or turn the font back to whatever colour it was. Meet your first draft mad rush story…

Tip: Try not to hit the Caps Lock key!

Here's a few of my own starter lines you are welcome to use as springboards:

1. I think I've just seen Smitz.
2. I was an apricot. So was Anna.
3. When Sammy Etherington woke, his head was a triangle.
4. The day the men came, Mama burned the soup and had to make it all over again.
5. Tommo you old Mutt, this is me.
6. Package on the doorstep…
7. There is, in Rue Carnot, a greengrocer's…
8. Section 1. It is mandatory to dress as a beekeeper…
9. One night in August, Ed's wife became an ant…
10. I have become a mote in my husband's eye.

PS – The blank screen idea is a brilliant one for busting writer's block. If you can't see what you are typing, you can't constantly edit, correct, sigh, etc.

If you don't work on a screen, put something over your notebook as you write underneath.

GAME 41 – PLACES WHERE

Here, you are relying on memory and detail.

Think of, and describe in as much detail as you can, these places. Spend time on whichever you choose. You might find that the details of the setting come back the longer you focus on the emotion that rises.

A place where you were happy for yourself

A place where you were happy for someone else

A place where you were unhappy for yourself

A place where you were unhappy for someone else

A place where you found something

A place where you lost something

And weave a story out of the emotion, the feeling you are left with, using your well- recalled place as the setting.

Or

Using scenes from something else you are working in, see if one of your vibrant new settings, created from a place of emotional truth, if you like, can enhance something already in existence by changing the backdrop.

GAME 42 – THE WRONG SUITCASE

Your character returns after a long flight, to find they have picked up what they thought was their suitcase off the baggage reclaim, but when they opened it, it wasn't theirs.

Take ten minutes to answer the following questions, either working in a first-person narrative or second, or third:

What's in it?

What do they do?

Spend another ten minutes on the following…

Who has their case?

What's in it?

What do they do?

What happens?

Do they meet?

Then what?

GAME 43 – SUPERSTITIONS

List as many superstitions as you can. Here are a few to start your list.

Bad luck :

Walking under a ladder

Looking in a broken mirror

Spilling salt

An upside-down horseshoe on a wall

Seeing a penny, letting it lie

Good luck :

Seeing a black cat walk across your path

Seeing a penny and picking it up

Finding a four-leafed clover

Seeing a shooting star

Carrying a bride over the threshold

Whatever character you might be working with, try giving them real superstitions and something that challenges them. How does it change them, and/or the story?

GAME 44 – THE LANGUAGE OF FLOWERS and STONES

Pick one flower (not literally) and spend time learning about it: Google the meanings, the associations, the symbolism attached, where it is found, whether it is endangered, whether or not is poisonous, find out what, if anything, eats it? Make notes, be aware of those facts that make you think 'Oh! Now I can work with that.'

Pick a stone (diamond, sapphire, garnet, etc) and again, spend time finding out about the meanings of that stone. Often, stones and flowers are attached to birthday months, for example. Maybe your character wears a particular-coloured stone because.... because what? Make notes. Listen to your reactions.

Why not pick two that don't seem to go together: eg, orchid/granite, stinging nettle/ruby?

Jump off and start swimming in whatever connections you make.

GAME 45 – JANUS WORDS

In Ancient Rome, Janus was the god of beginnings, entrances, gates, transitions, doorways, passages, frames, and endings. And probably a lot more. There are also Janus words, which are words that mean more than one thing – especially its own opposite.

Examples:

To cleave can mean to split apart or to unite.

Oversight can mean watchful care or an error of omission

Clip can mean to cut away or to link together.

Bolt can mean to hold together or to flee.

Buckle can mean to fasten together or to collapse under pressure.

Finished can mean completed or destroyed.

Dust (verb) can mean to cover with dust (in baking) or to take dust away (as in dusting).

Left can mean departed or remained behind.

Trim can mean to take away something or to add a decoration

Custom can mean one-off, specially made or common practice.

There are many more.

Your game is in two parts:

1. Choose a Janus word. Write two sentences, using the same word in each, with opposite meanings.

and

2. Using one sentence as the opening and the other as the ending, link them in a narrative.

See Part Two for an example.

GAME 46 – MORE LOST PROPERTY

London has also got a lost property treasure chest. Check back to Game 38 for the explanation, but it's fairly self-explanatory. Here's a list of some of the things found abandoned on the London Underground.

Who lost it? How? What happens next?

A jar of bull semen.

An urn of ashes

A stuffed boar's head.

A creepy doll dressed as a nun

A judge's wig

A toy gorilla in a wheelchair

A life-size Spiderman doll

An empty coffin

Find this list online and choose two things that don't seem to go together.

And make them go together. Collide them, in a tiny story or a tiny something.

GAME 47 – DOWN THE LOO

This game is to show you that I can find story ideas everywhere – and I mean everywhere – and so can you!

At St Pancras Station, in the ladies loo, there is a pictorial request not to flush anything other than the usual. The picture tells unsuspecting ladies not to flush the following:

A fish

A sock

A pair of glasses

An apple

Your game is to ignore the instruction and be the character who drops all four things down the loo at once.

Why on earth…?

Who on earth…?

You tell me!

GAME 48 – DROWNED AND FOUND

Global warming is having a devastating effect on water levels in rivers, lakes and reservoirs. They seem to be going down as sea levels rise. It's unfathomable, but for this, you need to try.

Time for the snorkel and mask. You are going to start finding things underwater.

Think rivers, canals, lakes and reservoirs. Think about a drop in water level, lower than it's ever been.

At first, the water is clear, and you can see what you think is …(what?). But as you swim, you churn up the water so it becomes cloudy. What's it like to swim through? Describe everything as you go.

You can no longer see the interesting thing you thought you saw, and you have to feel around with your fingers at the bottom. Do you have to dive over and over, or is it shallow? Describe it, how it feels. Tastes, even. Can you hear anything?

Your fingers touch something that isn't mud. What does it feel like? Describe it as much as you can. Can you pick it up? Do you have to find something to dislodge it? Does that make the water even cloudier?

What do you find?

How long has it been there?

Is it meant to be there, or is it something lost/hidden?

If so, who lost it?

When?

Keep going? There are stories here.

GAME 49 – NORTHERN LIGHTS WITH SOUNDTRACK

It has been discovered that the Aurora Borealis, The Northern Lights, are not just a visual phenomenon. They are accompanied by sounds. Many of these are too far away to be heard, but some, in the form of whistles and crackles, can sometimes be heard.

Find out more about it, if it feels like something that could be fascinating. Google. Take a look at the science.

What if…

Only a few people can hear them?

Who might they be? Children, not adults? The old, not the young? People who have specific beliefs?

Why can only they hear them?

Why can't everyone else?

How do they make people believe them?

Or do they?

What are the sounds saying?

What could happen?

Check Part Two for an example response that was unlike anything the writer had written before.

GAME 50 – SURREAL DEFINITIONS FROM THE FRENCH SURREALISTS

With thanks to Pascale Petit for introducing me to this one.

This is just the loveliest game. You need a supply of strips of paper, one for each word. Enough space to write a word on the left, and a one or two short sentence or two definition on the right. Play on your own, or in a group.

Here are some words to be going on with, although you will choose your own too.

Write these phrases, one per piece of paper, on the left:

A ship is

A violin is

A map is

A snake is

A mother is

A lily is

Snow is

A door is

A clown is

A storm is

A computer is

A castle is

A mirror is

A river is

A home is

A nightingale is

A tiger is

Smoke is

A sword is

The sun is

A story is

My thinking is

A ghost is

A hill is

Now, write an interesting definition of each word on the rest of the strip.

Eg: taking the first two words:

A ship is *a vessel that transports souls to far-off places.*

A violin is *the holder of the gift of pleasing sounds, in the right hands.*

Then, cut each strip after the word 'is', separating the definitions from the words, and make two piles: words and definitions. Then pick at random from each pile.

Swap your two examples above, and the sentences become:

A ship is the holder of the gift of sound, in the right hands

and

A violin is a vessel that transports souls to far-off places

Wonderful! Poetic metaphors at best and fascinating collisions that are almost logical.

See Part Two for a great list of surreal definitions of the long list above for you to use yourself.

GAME 51 – WORKING TO IMAGES iii

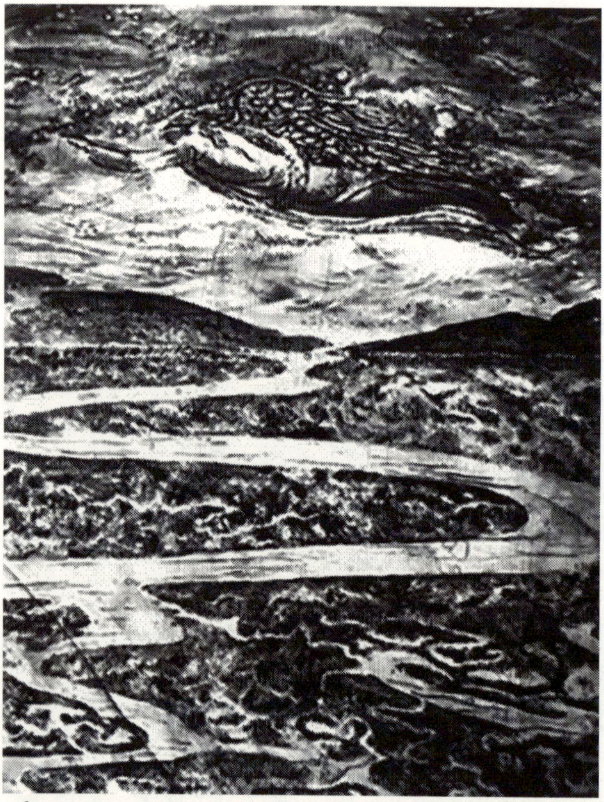

Transfiguration, a painting on antique glass, by Elizabeth Lamont.

Please Google a wonderful artist working in stained glass, by the name of Elizabeth Lamont. https://www.elizabethlamont.co.uk/index.html

On her home page, one down on the right, as I write this, you will see a short video of images and poetry featuring the stained glass installations she made in response to some of my poems, for an exhibition called Reflections.

Please don't start the video, unless it interests you, but focus on the first image: slowly, a blue, white and maroon angel emerges and floats above a hidden landscape. And let this image, or indeed any of the other ethereal artworks on her website inspire a 'something'. The image above is a poor reflection of her original. It needs to be seen in colour! However - the image above works too.

This image was inspired by a poem. In its turn, it and its fellows have inspired many other poems, and stories, too. It seems a good thing.

See Part Two for one such response.

PS: Images/works of visual art will inspire, but perhaps they need to be the right ones for us as individuals? I've tried a few in this book. Why not keep your eyes open for an image/painting/photo/stained glass window/ collage/statue/sculpture, etc that seems to be right for you?

GAME 51 and a half – GO ON, RANT, BREATHLESSLY

Hardly a game, just permission to rant. Get it off your chest. Let off steam. About anything you like – but keep it to 100 words, exactly.

You could make it a breathless rant, where you don't use full stops. Check out a brilliant example of breathless flash online on Smokelong Quarterly, called Next of Kin, by the talented Jo Gatford.

There's an example of a ranty 100-worder in Part Two..

PART TWO

RESPONSES TO SOME OF THE GAMES –

These games have, over a few years, at Grist to the Mill online evenings, or other workshops, inspired masses of new poems, new flashes, new short stories, and new 'writings' that are simply their own thing.

Some wonderfully generous writers who have worked with me in all kinds of workshops have offered their writing for this book. Sometimes edited, sometimes not. Sometimes the work has been worked on, polished and extended. They are generous enough to share their work with you just for the creative pleasure. Some have been published. Some nominated for awards. Most not. But they all have something in common - all of them have their creative roots firmly in one of the games here, in this book.

I've chosen these for that 'something' that sets the writing alight, when this reader engages with the words.

I hope they will inspire you too - so jump in and enjoy.

These are here to celebrate our creativity. All of us.

RESPONSE TO CRICKET 1

This was written online during a Grist to the Mill session. It's unedited.

Day 32
by Frances Hay

On the calendar, the next day didn't exist. It was the invisible extra day designed specifically for invisibility. Only those drawn to nothingness could make an appointment, feeling sorry to lose friends and even enemies, on a day that was like no other.

Day 32 was full of noises but the most important was the signal—as mournful as the curlew's cry, a sign of sadness as, limb by limb, parts of us disappeared into nothingness.

We'd all booked into the day, but like wary guests in a strange hotel, we didn't meet each other's eyes and, in any case, soon there were no eyes to meet.

Your senses are quite strange when you're invisible. As bits of my eyes joined up with nothingness, any sense of them transformed. The poplar trees that guarded the boundary of the grounds narrowed into tall, hazy twigs, then faded to merge with the foggy air.

The trouble was, the less I could count on a bounded world, a world of geometric if not algebraic rules – the seedier I began to feel. In the receding world of things, I felt unsteady; I could only see the aura of a migraine I would not be able to escape.

I tore my eyes away from the grounds, looking down at the nubby upholstery on the cushioned swing seat. But then that faded, and I could not see any support for my limbs—and now I could not see any semblance of legs beneath my kneecaps. This was a kind of hell, trapped in the body that I remembered but was ceasing to exist.

I have always trusted in science, not other people. But I don't know how to trust in a world without Newtonian rules, without Euclidean axioms. I still do not know how to live in a world where I am invisible, not just to those in power, but even to myself.

RESPONSE TO CRICKET 2

This is from Lottie Clark, who worked with me at Gladfic, a week's writing course at the gorgeous Gladstone's Library. She says:

"What I notice now is that your choice of words beginning with P seems to have got into my subconscious mind and I also used a lot of words beginning with P – more than would normally occur to me! Some words will fit in seamlessly, no tweaks of tenses required. Other words will send your ideas careering off in a different direction. It's the verbal equivalent of limbering up and, every time I play, I'm reminded that I love it! I never know what I will write and so I surprise myself with rogue surfers committing murder or a stream of consciousness-style Japanese monk choosing a motorbike. Sometimes my Word Cricket exercises are lyrical nonsense. Sometimes there's the germ of a good idea, or the plot or characters appear almost fully formed. Occasionally, they just don't work – and that's okay, too. The goal is simply to loosen things up and creep up on inspiration without making a big deal out of it!"

Ps & Qs at the Persimmon Coffee House
By Lottie Clark

I couldn't stand her – the way she latched onto every conversation and subverted it to her own ends. She'd first appeared in my café a few months ago – a domineering woman who sat at an adjacent table and talked incessantly at me as I tried to read my newspaper. Each day thereafter, the calm sanctuary of the Persimmon Coffee House was shattered by her arrival, the bellowed greetings to all and sundry, and the pantomime of her divesting scarves, garments and carrier bags. She was determined to broadcast her every thought regardless of (or, perhaps, oblivious to) anyone else who happened to be speaking.

As time wore on, I varied my routine: a Saturday afternoon here, a Monday morning there. No matter what I did, she turned up, took her position and, within minutes, the din and hubbub was intolerable. Even if she left before I did, a cloying scent of overripe pineapple lingered. My late wife had worn perfume – something elegant, sparingly applied. I'd never known how much the smell of one woman could permeate and fill a room with her latent presence.

So, I began avoiding the Persimmon and sought out alternatives – without much success or satisfaction. I've always prided myself on being a patient man but after a month of exile, I felt aggrieved. No other café roasted their own coffee beans or provided daily newspapers. No other café was so well-lit with comfortable and capacious armchairs, sturdy tables and pleasant staff. From the outset of my retirement, the Persimmon Coffee House had become my home from home, particularly after my wife died. The loss of the Persimmon destabilised my plumbline and, at times. I feared I would sink.

Had anyone noticed my absence?

I rather suspected that the Persimmon itself was in trouble as familiar faces increasingly showed up in other cafés. And in passing by the Persimmon one afternoon, I saw it to be empty.

Such joy in a perfect espresso!

I sank gratefully into an armchair and opened a pristine newspaper. One glorious sip of coffee and then – she bustled in, all tra-la-la-la and haven't-seen-you-in-a-long-time. Quite sure you aren't dead?

Pants, pants, pants. By the big-bottomed bloomers of Queen Victoria, how did this woman do it? That is, how did she show up within minutes of my arrival? She must live nearby. Perhaps she has a vantage view of the Persimmon doorway? Yet for all her prattle, I had no idea if she had family, hobbies or lived in a single room, a flat or a house.

I finished my coffee and left the café, striding off in the opposite direction to the way I believed she came from. I lurked in a doorway several shops up from the Persimmon. I'd not waited long before she also left the café. I followed her downhill at a discreet distance. Her house – a small mid-Victorian terrace that spilt onto the pavement – was further than I'd estimated, but it was on my regular route to the Persimmon. Despite her airs and graces, the evidence before me suggested penny-pinching. Paint was peeling off the front door and the red brickwork was in want of re-pointing. I risked peeping through the front window – cheap furnishings, repro prints and tired wallpaper. Maybe it was rented.

I sized up the front door lock. It was pretty standard. I walked to the end of the terraced row, relieved to see the usual small back yards with gated access to a narrow passageway. It was always handy to have a back exit in case of fire. A mad scheme had popped into my head. I went home and late into the night I perspired over the soldering of delicate wires and metal oddments to create the mechanism that I needed.

The next day, just before dawn, I returned to her house. It was child's play to slip the lock, although I wasn't trying to break in. I meant to jam the door fast. The process was noiseless and swiftly executed. I was back home before my bedsheets had had time to get cold, Later, I sauntered past her front window on my way to the Persimmon in time for their opening. I had decided to treat myself to breakfast as well as a leisurely perusal of the papers. I was halfway through my second coffee when I glanced through the window and spotted the locksmith's van caught up in traffic. She wouldn't be long, so it was time to depart. I repeated my ruse towards the end of the week, then once or twice in subsequent weeks. It was wonderful to regain the Persimmon, even for a short time. And other customers seemed to be returning when she was not in occupation, holding court, like an imperious, beady-eyed Plantagenet queen.

I knew the game was up when, on returning from town, I noticed a shiny, secure new lock on her door. I braced myself for the inevitable but to my knowledge she never came back to the Persimmon. There was an interesting story that caught my attention in the local paper: "Retiring locksmith finds the key to love" and there was a nice photograph of the newlyweds.

I raised my coffee cup and toasted them both.

RESPONSE TO CRICKET 3

This was written on an Arvon Online course.

Amelioration
By Tessa Bide

She stopped the car and turned around.
"If you two carry on fighting, I will drive this car off that bridge. Do you understand me?"
Her tinnitus hammered into her skull and her left eye pulsated.
The two small children in the back of the car were silent in the darkness. The woman took a deep breath to calm her cantering heart. "If you make a racket or distract me, we might be spotted and you will be taken", she reminded them.
Acid drops of fear trickled down her neck and she gripped the wheel tighter. Her white knuckles glowed.
The children understood. The source of their argument scuttled off into the night and they were left sitting in silence.
"Good. Now. We're going through another checkpoint in a moment, so you need to put the blanket over you and be quiet."
An ammonia smell pierced the woman's nostrils, sharp and unpleasant. A reflection of the children's fear, seeping into the car's upholstery. She should've stopped for a toilet break, but it was too dangerous.
She rolled down the window.

"Where are you travelling to today?", the soldier carrying a huge, monochrome gun asked her at the check point.
"Just to my mothers in Delsby. I am a Blade. Here are my papers."
"Anyone else on board? Any minors?"
"No, they're both in the amelioration programme", she replied, keeping her features neutral and calm.
"Good. I'll allow you passage for 24 hours. Any longer and we will know."

He waved her through. She pulled off and started driving over the bridge. Acrid sweat seeped through the pyjamas she was still wearing under her large woolen coat.

They had made it through another one. She felt the children's relief radiating from the blanket in the back seat. They were one step closer to freedom.

RESPONSES TO CRICKET 4

At the Flash Fiction Festival, 2022, the atmosphere was wonderful. It was the first face to face get together of so many of the flash community since Covid. I was invited to run a workshop and offered a game of Word Cricket, if they'd like. They did like. We delivered the game to the whole assembly as an ice breaker, entitling it The Biggest Game of Word Cricket in the Whole Wide World. (Of course, if you know different, let me know!)

Here are two contributions written in that fast and furious ten minutes… the first, by Roberta Beary, was first published, tidied for typos only, in Litro. She said: "*…hats off to you for your prompts Vanessa and your whole Word Cricket concept. It sure worked for this first-timer.*"

Word Salad
by Roberta Beary

On my doorstep, a package. On the package no name but I'm pretty sure it's from my mom, even though she died 10 years ago today – in one sense a messy death – the other a success according to the surgeon who said her hip was healing beautifully – the messy bit was her organs shut down over 24 hours.

I recognize her handwriting as if she'd written it yesterday – her favorite purple pen too – along with the little hearts over the i's and the slant of the pen to the right – hold on – one time in Johannesburg I wouldn't eat the ice cream she wanted to get – I thought it would bring out the lions and Mom laughed and called me a looney bird – she called me that right up until she stopped speaking and I had to put her in the dementia ward – instead of smelling like Chanel No 5 she stank of ammonia – from when the ward sisters forgot to change her Laura Ashley nightie – hospital gown – the place was none too clean and I'd idle away the odd hour crushing ants in the washbasin – her frowning the whole time – looney bird her lips mouthed – she thought I couldn't make it out but I knew – the package might be a bomb – I'd not put it past her.

I'm shivering – like someone stepped over my grave – or hers – the ticking ticking ticking – tiny hearts over the i's little bells ringing a call to prayer for all the bad children now caretakers who dot their i's with tiny hearts crying – I'm here – I matter – never say die she'd say – my one A+ in history not enough to please her – or was it never give in – a magnet on the fridge from the shop by Blenheim Castle – how I couldn't drive the car with its stick shift and she showed me the gear box working it perfectly, her hands like the surgeon who fixed her hip – that long slow climb up to her bed he said shouldn't be a problem anymore – she's as good as new – but the ward GP said she'd only a few hours left and the surgeon skedaddled and sent in his female assistant to tell me again how beautifully Mom's hip was healing – and by morning she was gone – at least I thought she was until the package with her handwriting – so like mine – right down to the tiny little hearts dotting the I's.

And another, to show how different responses can be, using the same words.

The Musical Box
by Sarah Oakes

On my doorstep, a package. On the package, no name. All there was were a series of odd runes, swirling in deep purple across the parcel, and an address in Johannesburg. Curious, I took it inside. It was as light as an ant, although the box was larger than my coffee table.

There was no seam, no edge to tear it open with. I sifted through my cluttered coffee table, looking for the scissors that had surely been there yesterday. Perhaps I could pierce the carboard with the scissors, like a knife slicing through shell.

As I did, there was a sound, from the box. A single lone note, that sung from the depths of the cardboard, that turned into a tune, C to D to E to F to G, until a series of coughs cut the scale short. The box shimmered, the cardboard illuminated by a shade of ammonia, like mustard seeds and dying suns. Something moved inside the box. Something was in trouble. Something shivered.

There had to be a way to open it. I looked again, but the only key was the runes. Fingers fumbling, I traced the odd letters and characters, pronouncing them as best I could. For once, I was glad Lord Eldritch was such a stickler for vowels and consonants. I read the whole box, and as I reached the end of one particular sentence, the runes parted at the top of the box. A carpet of blank space rippled outwards as the box shivered again, before it was filled with staves of music, an old melody of secrets and wonder. I sang it as best as I could, although there were no words. And something it sang in reply, a question-and-answer refrain, in pianissimo, barely audible but keenly felt, from inside the box. I had never seen anything like it. Lord Eldritch always said the world was full of strange magic. Now I realised what he meant.

As I finished the tune, the box opened, with a click and a chorus. The box was lined with soft satin, cradling the creature at the bottom. I gazed in wonder. At the bottom, was a beautiful being of old magic, saffron body struggling to breathe, wings burnt and broken, one leg at an odd angle, a harmony of gashes and gunshots reverberating across her chest. The eyes were shut, but a few notes issued from her lips, a choked chord. There was a faint glow, an amethyst shade, as her heart tried to beat, close to death. A Fae. No one had seen one in centuries. And now, here was one, on my doorstep.

Carefully, I cradled her, gently lifting her from the box. I arranged some cushions on the sofa and laid her against them. I knew what my magic was for now. I spoke a spell, emerald light caressing saffron fur, as the gashes on her chest vanished and she started to smile, to breathe a bit more. I would take her in, care for her, look after her. Tomorrow, she would be a little better, and we would take it from there, one step at a time.

RESPONSES TO CRICKET 5

This comes from Diana Wallsgrove, who worked with me on the 'Just Write!' course at Petersfield Museum.

She apologised that her piece was 'silly', saying: "*I found that the opening phrase sparked an idea. Then I had to be open to the challenge of fitting the words in as they appeared. They sometimes took me in unexpected directions. One challenge, typing it up, was resisting the urge to 'improve' it. I resisted!*"

To which I say, 'Hey. Never apologise for a just born first draft. Or a second draft, and on and on. We have to let ourselves make messy drafts, or we have work that is tough as old boots…'

I've always hated flying
by Diana Wallsgrove

I've always hated flying – the strain on the arms, well, wings – the need to find the thermals, read them, bank, turn, swerve, and then when to flap. It's not easy, not easy at all.

So, this one day, I was over a poppy field, glistening red in the sun, and I must have got distracted because one minute I was up there, high in the sky, master of all I surveyed, yadda, yadda, an albatross on a sight-seeing tour of Southern England, and the next – whang! Someone had shot a ruddy great crossbow – not meant kindly, no, the opposite – a vicious attack, designed to kill. Got me in the wing, it did.

"Bigamy!" I exclaimed – just the first thing that came into my head – no such thing for us. Mate for life, we do.

The bolt, shaft or whatever, fortunately for me, had missed my vital parts but one wing was knackered, frankly. I hopped a bit, feeling unstable, with the arrow stuck in. I grabbed the end in my beak and pulled. Relief. It dislodged but blood came out too, marring my feathers. How would I get to Cairo now? That's where I was headed.

Rest a bit, I thought, gather your wits.

I settled down. I wasn't a coward but when I looked up, I was scared to see buzzards circling. Big, they looked, bigger than me, some of 'em. They were black as coaldust against the bright sky. I stretched, flapped. This would be an unforgettable experience – and possibly my last.

And another from Andy Thomsen, also at Petersfield Museum

I've always hated flying
by Andy Thomsen

I've always hated flying. Or so I said. Actually, it was the crashing bit. It wasn't even that of course, it was not being able to get off. What if I lost control? Went mad? The embarrassment! Nowhere to hide.

The woman opposite was wearing a tatty old poppy, faded and wilting. She looked terrified. By way of a joke, and to engage with her, I asked her if her name was Poppy? 'No, it's Rose'. No flicker of a smile. 'I'm Albert', I said. 'It's always been a bit of an albatross around my neck, to be honest'. The humour fell flat as we began to descend…

Rose now looked kindly at me, in sympathy at having to own such a sense of humour. 'I like having my head in the clouds', I persevered. 'I'm just winging it', she said, 'that's bigamy….' 'Big of you? How?'. She let that one pass, then said 'May I sit next to you? You can hold my hand for when my head gets ripped off'. Remembering Tom Lehrer, and his hostage to fortune jokes, I agreed. Mentioning his name, she offered me some peanuts. 'Wrong song', I said, but the horse had already bolted. 'Stable?'. 'No, not really, but who is?'. And so we started telling our stories, as scared passengers do, as evidence that we still exist.

'Last saw him in Cairo' said a voice from the row behind us. 'Made a fortune!'. We smiled in a newfound intimacy, as if we understood the nuance of his boast. 'Probably a reprobate…' I ventured. 'A coward. Running away from his wife. Almost certainly'. A screech of tyres and a puff of smoke brought us back to the reality that we had finally landed. Back in the land of smog and coal dust. But it felt like home. Our first journey together had been unforgettable, just great. We'd landed.

RESPONSES TO CRICKET 7

This is from a Grist to the Mill session.

Trudi Taylor from the US says: "*a 3,300-word story became a 308 word flash! Somehow, the shortened length gives the tale more punch. A lady attorney in a twinset and pearls once told me about her first beer at a swanky wine bar in North Carolina. I embellished but will be forever grateful for the idea. The Burns word cricket reminded me to dust it off. Using the term 'beastie' added some authenticity, as the Appalachian mountains are home to many Scots.*"

My First Beer Thanks to Crazy Uncle Ted
by Trudi Taylor

One momentous day in my twelfth year, around twenty-five kin circled the yard with shotguns, rifles, and a BB gun. Always concerning when beered-up, I had pulled on my sissy-orange vest and kept behind my Crazy Uncle Ted. Bobbie Junior, at the I'll-live-forever age of nine, dropped a firecracker into one of many groundhog tunnels threatening our homestead with collapse.

Wowsa!

The earth swarmed with varmints two feet long and weighing as much as my gran's pocketbook.

Crazy Uncle Ted let off some shots, missed, reloaded, aimed, and the kick from the shotgun knocked him into me.

"What you doing back there, girlie?"

"Watching them die," I said with the proper amount of crazy.

And then a groundhog made a run for it. My uncle racked his shotgun.

"Stand back, this one's mine."

I scurried back, trampling Mama's prize azaleas. Crazy Uncle Ted went eyeball-to-eyeball with the granddaddy of all groundhogs. He fired.

Ch-chunk!

Part of Uncle Ted's work boot still containing three toes catapulted through the air. The groundhog stopped, looked at us, and I could've sworn the beastie laughed.

"Well, I'll be damned," Crazy Ted exclaimed.

While my uncle reloaded, the beastie turned, making a beeline straight for me. I hoisted myself into a magnolia, closed my eyes, and prayed to Sweet Baby Jesus to deliver us from the Plague of Groundhogs. Uncle Ted, Clorox-white and goofy-eyed from blood loss, blasted the tree with buckshot. The varmint taunted us.

I hustled over. "Gimme that." Aimed, and the groundhog splattered former blue-ribbon azaleas.

That night, Crazy Uncle Ted gave me my first beer. "You ain't no angel."

I placed the ice-cold Bud against the black eye from the shotgun kick.

"That's a badge of honor," the family said and made room for me at the grown-ups' table. I pulled the tab on the beer and took a sip.

And another, from Jo Russ. This one and the one before just show, quite superbly, how you don't have to be slave to the words - especially weird ones. Just let the game take you…

Best Laird Plan.
(After To a Mouse, by Robbie Burns)
by Jo Russ

On turning twice she lay in the hay and noticed a twisting. She turned and saw that a thistle had pierced the roof, exposing the morning.
It sprung up with a bristling tongue under fascist flat-top, staring.

Her best-laid nest, curved by her stomach, still warm to touch.
Safe, she thought, after the harvest. A young life's work, a hatch against the thatcher.
But the walls began to cave around the jousting alien with flipper blades splayed, made for precise demolition; standing to attention with tyrannous precision.

The mouse drew up onto her hind legs, poised.
Her pink nose twitched to the rhythm of her fast and furious heart.
Her nose and whisker lifted in a snifter to the silhouette bouncer in the doorway *She* built: robust, expecting *her* to stand in its threshold.
"Move!" she tried, "This is mine!"
But still it stood, silent.
Foreboding.
Armed and fully-loaded.

Her exit was plugged.
Her escape plan tugged away by the thistle's grip.
Not tractor or cat
But a war of the wilds, an alien trap
She shifted,
Then still

She waited defiant and radiant in pink gloves and pumps; eyes twinkling hazel.
Her sharp, efficient teeth were ready for battle.

In other worlds the faraway field was soon to be flat
The burly boy-farmers whistled a Combine chorus, familiar and unfathomable, warm and winsome.
The bunting whipped and cracked under the unusual gust in complements of orange, green and red; faded from bygone fetes and sun storage.

She banked and rolled away from the dust-bowl of the village.
Moving on again to make another, better laid plan.

RESPONSES TO CRICKET 9

I am including two example responses for this game, so you can see two different approaches - how one writer has used all the words, and the second has riffed off the opening phrase and ended up with a complete, polished short story draft. As I keep saying - no one is checking. Anything goes. Just write…

Firstly then, a response from a Grist to the Mill session, containing all the words:

They were walking straight towards me
By Liz Churchill

They were walking straight towards me carrying parrot food. It was dripping through their fingers like sand: sunflower seeds, sesame seeds (I think?), and what looked like dried red chilies – which I suppose made sense though I'd never really considered what parrots ate before. Amazing birds, I have to admit. The way their feathers look drenched in primary colours of ink, like a freshly painted passion project of a young child. The tropical feeling those birds give, even in the night, even in the shadows, even in this grotty, piss-smelling alleyway.

Something glinted in one of the men's hands. I noticed it that moment in a gasp of moonlight. Was it a screwdriver? What was he doing with it? What was he going to do? I took a step back, instinctively.

I felt my back pocket – the chocolate bar was still there but, warmed by my nervous buttocks, it was beginning to soften and melt. My bowels made a violent threat. I thought of the jungle where those parrots should be. I pictured the lush undergrowth, imagined the chirping, cawing, hothouse of creatures. The myriad feathers deafening in their flight. The smells of exotic pollen brought me back to myself. It's not a good time to be losing your marbles now, mate, I chastised myself.

One of the men stepped forward, his smile like a slither of shorn off toenail. He had a sinful face. He opened his mouth and said, "Who's a pretty Polly? Who's a pretty Polly?"

And that's when the parrots arrived – fanned out in the sky like the shape of Spain.

And second, a response from a writer on the Petersfield Museum course - a polished short story, which riffs off that first half-line:

Reading other People's Books
by Jane Dunster

He has a dog under his arm. When he last came into the shop, it was cardboard boxes - flattened, but still unwieldy. His coat is done up with what in a less urban environment might have been bailer twine and his rheumy eyes hang down at the corners, as though overladen. Hair foams in unlikely crests of grey, brown, nicotine around his head.

"Rowing boats," he announces to Matt, who happens to be on till. Matt is wearing another of his seemingly inexhaustible array of comic character, obscure musician, or science fiction-related t-shirts. He has a slightly droopy blonde moustache and I feel there is a reason he does not wear Asterix the Gaul. He glances at his protein shake. "Excuse me?"

"D'you have any books on rowing boats?"

"Well I don't think..."

"We might have Swallows and Amazons?" I offer, extracting a copy that has been on the shelf for quite some time.

"Sailing," Mr Heath counters decidedly. The little dog (Jack Russell? Borderline Collie?) looks around with an air of intelligence. They probably couldn't be palmed off with Three Men in a Boat, either. Close to, there's a sour, yeasty scent I don't actually find unpleasant. Like herb beer brewing, perhaps. In a dank cellar, Mr Heath ferments his own eau de cologne.

He changes tack, if you can do that in an imaginary rowing boat. "Saturday Morning Cinema. Tarzan. Flash Gordon." He weaves across to Music, Film and TV. Just how old is this man? Is there any connection between these apparent interests, or have his thoughts just stuttered on to them? Electricity. Genius. Seizure. Stroke.

Stroke. Brings us back to rowing.

Mr Heath has been coming to the shop longer than I've been volunteering here. Our manager, Alasdair, always greets him with liberal respect. Alasdair is not here. He is on a City Break in Berlin with his second wife. Alasdair smells of lemon, also not unpleasantly. Matt, as Deputy Manager, is opening up every day but Friday in his absence and the protein shake is an emblem of his breakfastless discontent.

"I wonder who's looking after them?"

Matt doesn't look up, for fear Mr Heath quizzes him about Ballroom Dancing or Plumbing or Eighteenth Century Poetry. "Who?"

"Alasdair's children." Alasdair has five children: two with his late wife, two with his later wife and a stepson I can't quite place. I've babysat for him quite a few times, that's how I started here. When I go to his house (the children are always asleep) I can lose myself in Peter Scupham and Marcel Proust and RD Laing. He must have noticed me looking at the books, he knew I was ready to try working again and suggested I come in for a few shifts.

Matt shrugs. Now he is watching the dog, but he doesn't want the dog to see him doing it. Jellyfish would outspine Matt. You can see, what with the politely delayed exodus of customers, that Mr Heath's arrival has not exactly elevated the ambiance. Matt won't tell him to leave though. I wouldn't either but then I'm on Alasdair's wavelength. He talks to me when we're on shift together.

Matt mutters something about needing to ring Neil and heads down the circular stair to the basement. You have to turn a tighter spiral than you might have thought because there are stacks of books piled all down one side. I wonder what Alasdair is doing. Perhaps he and Helen are taking cold beer (non-alcoholic) and cured meats in an enclosed garden.

Should I start that Christopher Isherwood omnibus I was saving for the window display in Pride Month?

Eventually, Mr Heath shuffles back to the desk. He pushes a book towards me. It is an unshowy seventies paperback, which Alasdair established was of low commercial value, although he did say that it might be worth hanging on to and only reluctantly surrendered it into stock. Clearly Mr Heath, whatever his disparate concerns, has taste.

He furtles deep into a coat pocket on the opposite side to the dog, pulling out a roll of something crumpled that turns out when separated to be banknotes. I ring it through for him and as he leaves he puts the change in the tin, even though we are a charity anyway. The dog yawns. Mr Heath gently strokes the soft hair between its eyebrows. He holds the dog's gaze patiently, chuntering to it as they leave the shop together. Its name seems to be Lowri, which I know is Welsh for Laura.

When one of the other volunteers comes in a little later I go to take my lunch break. Downstairs Matt is going through boxes. Neil brings in half a van full of books at a time and Alasdair and Matt sift through them for anything not obviously mainstream. Matt appears to have discovered a photographic alphabet of naked and somewhat hairy individuals which is printed on high gloss paper.

"Mr Heath bought that book Alasdair liked. The one you said should have won the Booker in 1974."

"Going to have to recycle this one I think." He slides the nudes into a bag. Pulp, or maybe private collection.

I agitate my instant soup. A mistake, even with the croutons. It's as though they solidify out of something that wasn't really there to begin with. Alasdair has a whole seam of books on his bedroom landing about psychedelic drugs and primal therapy and the absent father. His children obviously haven't discovered them yet, I suppose they will migrate to the bedroom eventually. Or maybe Helen doesn't like them.

I suppose Mr Heath must be homeless, or squatting somewhere. I wish I could be generous and kind to him without silently congratulating myself. I wish I could be properly good, like Alasdair.

Matt is still assaying. Mr Heath says many things, he buys many books. Does he read them? The things he says are melting, drifting away from one another as ice floes in a warming sea. Are there still vast unbroken sheets to wander, or perhaps the words float out and freeze solid, forge different routes?

"Matt, how old is Mr Heath? I mean he looks…but then I suppose…"

Matt does not shrug. Instead he stills himself and looks right at me so I have to look away. "Mr Heath? Older than he looks. One of those people who just go on….despite everything. Alasdair knew him when he were a kid."

So he shifts in my mind. A prematurely raddled man but one whose continued existence proves that sometimes we stay on merely by chance. Alasdair told me once that he had lost his father when he was still at school; it was the unlit corner of an anecdote to which he never returned.

A paperback on top of one of the stacks catches my eye. It gives me those goose walking over your grave feelings. I have never seen that edition before, but there is something familiar. It has a horrible orange cover with a looming skull. It is about the last day in the life of an alcoholic.

Sometimes when I am there in his house I look at the books Alasdair is reading so we can talk about them when we work together. He always has six or seven by his bed because like me he doesn't watch much television and has room for several strands in his mind.

And above his bed is a shelf with his special books, the ones he has not passed on to his children, the Anthony Powell his wife gave him the Christmas before she got diagnosed and a first edition Alan Garner inscribed 'Alasdair, may you always see the light, love Dad.'

There is another, a hardback, inscribed by the same hand, but unsigned. It is bound in ash grey, bloodshot with red lettering. Under the Volcano, Malcom Lowry. Lowry, not Lowri. Lost, not dead, not forgotten. Someone has written the price in pencil on the flyleaf. They have pressed a little too hard. I know from experience you can never really erase those marks.

RESPONSES TO CRICKET 10

This is from writer ***Sylvia Petter,*** who used this game to start a new crime novel.

Here's Chapter One.

The middle of the city is no place for an apprentice cook to get lost and not find the hotel where his apprenticeship is due to start. It´s not really the place for him to get his bearings, but it´s also not the place to get anxious – he´ll get anxious enough when he has to serve his first dishes. He won´t be able to run off like a thief then, and he mustn´t do so now. He has to take a deep breath, look around, get his bearings, even ask someone the way to Hotel Bristol where his apprenticeship is due to start. No, he mustn't be anxious. That will come.

Now where was that map?

Carl Süsskind suddenly thought of the partridge he'd cooked for his mother's birthday. She´d been astounded.

"Where did you get that?" she´d asked.

"On sale at Lidl. They even had a small pear tree," he'd said with a wink.

He had to move on. He was running now and saw his reflection in the shop window. It was really a mirror and men would stop in front of it and adjust their ties, women would fluff up their hair. It was next to the flower shop where the honeybee buzzed. It wasn't a real bee, of course, just one of those drone things, a gimmick to attract attention. It even had a name.

Quite guessable. "Honeybee" was marked on a sign planted into a flowerpot. It was behind glass. Like in a prison when they interview culprits, thieves, murderers, even before they get their confessions.

Confession? When was the last time? He hadn't been for ages. He jumped.

Crikey! That motorbike nearly knocked him over. He had to pay attention to where he was going and not daydream. This was going to be his new life. If he got in. No more police work for him.

It was that woman who had also encouraged him to do an apprenticeship as a cook. They'd been manipulating him back at the Cure place, trying to get him to play the line, the party line. But then the party was gone and there he was with nowhere to go and she´d said: "People have to eat. Learn how to cook!"

He'd looked out to the grass in front of the Clinic and felt she had a point there. A cow was munching. They had to eat. So did people. And so now he was in the big city, not lost, but still trying to find the way to his apprentice brothers – maybe there'd be sisters, too – one never knew these days.

Women played such big roles in his life: his mother, his boss lady, Sabrina Neuling, one of the Cure patients, he wondered if the head cook at the Bristol was a woman. That would be the ticket, he thought.

But a man had responded to his application, and he'd been told to report to Mr Fritz Happenstantz, Head Cook at Bristol Hotel, Vienna.

And another, from the same prompts, underlining how vastly different we all are, creatively, as well as everything else:

SHEPHERD'S PIE
*by Maria Sang*er

In the middle of the city, the people walked absent-mindedly past the shops, not looking in the windows, but they stared ahead intent on reaching the stations. They were just a statistic – each person one of millions journeying back to the place called home.

Worst of it was when they arrived at the stations: it was the first time that there were no trains or buses or cars, just a strange contraption no one had ever seen before. Most did not feign surprise or alarm, nor even frown. All except one that is.

George Spicer was his name. With his red corduroys and stripey shirt he stood out from the greyness of the crowd. As he followed the person in front of him, he was convinced a thief must have stolen the people's expressions or identities. He could not ascertain how it could be possible – it was more than his brain could accommodate at the end of a long day when all he wanted to do was to go home and eat his wife Bertha's, shepherd's pie and have a cool ale. He was sure someone in the office had mentioned something odd happening earlier in the day. Some freak weather condition or perhaps an alien shower had come down while he'd been working at the computer. Come to think of it there had been a strange yellow light in the office when Mary Besant had been talking about her new pet partridge. It had been four o'clock when he had looked at his watch. But then George couldn't remember what else she'd been harping on about. He had stared out of the window onto the greyness of the afternoon, at the grey buildings of Chancery Lane and the grey cars and the grey people, and his eyes had blurred. Yes, that must have been it. How he wished he had looked in the mirror earlier to check he was still the same person. If only he could ring Bertha to let her know he would be late, but his mobile was no longer in the pockets of his jacket. Nor were the pockets in his jacket. Nor was the jacket his.

A sweat passed over him in the throng. Why on Earth was no one talking now? He grabbed the arm of the person walking alongside him. 'Please help me,' he said. 'What is going on?' But the stranger said nothing, continuing to walk with an ant-like precision and purposefulness. He began to worry. Prison would be like this; only they'd be carrying trays with yellow food and coloured dish water for tea. Not nearly so tasty as Bertha's shepherd. His mouth salivated at the thought.

The people in front didn't look behind. He must be at least fifty rows back. One was already climbing onto the contraption, and he wondered how long it would be before it was his turn. Bertha would definitely be worried now. He'd have to make it up to her. And then, for the first time, he saw the thing. It wasn't exactly like a motorbike, but what looked to be a strange bicycle with a parachute.

And then the next one took off and twisted its handlebars around as it soared above his head, but it was still some way off and he couldn't quite see who was driving it. Still his watch said four o'clock. He shook his arm, but the battery must have died. It must be nearer to seven, he thought.

He would miss his dinner at this rate. The woman in front was wearing a purple hat, and a sprig of lavender hit his nostrils because he stepped too close to her. It reminded him of his school days when the drama teacher had scolded him for being too late to class. She wore lavender too. He groaned and tutted, trying to squeeze through the crowds, but no one would budge. Blow it! He squatted down and shouted, 'Aliens, Aliens,' but no one reacted. He crawled along on his hands and knees. No one tried to stop him. Still, he kept going until he found himself at the front of the queue.

How elegant! The bicycle had a brass frame with a highly polished bell, and an automaton spun jerkily round and placed a sticker on George's jacket as he stood up. There was a code written on it: GS64. It even had his initials. Then the robot scanned George with a handheld device and watched him as he climbed onto the frame and clutched the handlebars. He gave George a shove and in seconds the bicycle was airborne – it was similar to something he had seen once in the Science Museum as a boy – except that was the balloon of the Courvoisier brothers. The machine was cruising at quite a speed now. He wondered which direction it would take him home. His taste buds were working overtime now and he was feeling ravenous. After the shepherd's pie, he'd have apple pie and custard and a coffee with mints. Yes, he was thankful there had been no need to buy a ticket. This journey was living beyond expectations.

Still he was rising. He thought he saw the River Ouse that undulated through the county of Bedford where he lived and even thought he saw his house with the swimming pool and stables, but then the bicycle dived down and was blown by the wind in a strange circular direction. As he was swept along, it dawned on him that he no longer recognised the landscape. He half-glimpsed colours of red and brown all around him. Still, he was hurled through the atmosphere at such a speed, and the vaporous gasses made him feel nauseous, so he closed his eyes. He didn't quite fancy the shepherd's pie now. He'd tell Bertha he'd eat it later. All night long, the bicycle continued to fly past the strange yellow world that went up even higher than the clouds and the Moon and the stars.

RESPONSE TO GAME 11

Don't just mention the egg cup - throw it at someone...

Working at a residential weekend for writers with The Writing Mill in a gorgeous farmhouse in Devon, for one workshop I put together a selection of items gleaned on walks over the Great War battlefields: some shrapnel, one or two bullets, a buckle, and several buttons. I added an old cigarette packet bought at a junk shop. I asked my writers to take a look, handle the items if they wanted, and then write. Think sideways.

Of course, writers think sideways – it's in our genes, after all – and I expected anything from letters from the front, to poems, to historical narratives, to memoir, non-fiction... you name it.

One writer came up with something really different. You need to know that she is very knowledgeable about geology, knows rocks of all kinds, fossils, too. Here are the notes she kindly dug out for me, where you can clearly see her thought processes.

All she wrote at that session were short notes. She explained that the shrapnel, which came from artillery shells, had connected her to another sort of shell. She wrote notes as follows:

> *Notes to self*
> *by Dev Jaffe*
>
> We, the intelligent species kill with fossils in the field
> Belemnites and echinoids wait to be unearthed
> The past is the key to the present
> But what use is knowledge when it leaves fossils in the field?

Later, in her own time, the images and her connections continued to work on her. Sadly, there is only space here to share short examples of the two pieces I have. Each is a good few thousand words long, develops character neatly and has a great narrative arc. They are all hung on quotes about different rocks, which act as metaphor. They could easily be the first stab at a collection of short stories.

Serpentine (extract)
by Dev Jaffe

(Serpentine: a rare example of metamorphism. This rock is so named because it resembles snakeskin.)

Sleep, that ever-elusive bed-mate had evaded her again. Through ill-fitting curtains, she spied features forming in the first light. A bird she didn't couldn't identify led the dawn chorus. With morning hair and heavy limbs, Annie moulted her sleeping bag, slithered into jogging bottoms and eased on her ancient hoodie. This outfit alone would have caused a serious eruption, but he was nowhere near to explode.

While she glided out into the dawn and headed in the direction she presumed would take her to the sea, the guidebook words echoed round her frazzled mind, 'The clear turquoise waters at Kynance Cove on the Lizard Peninsula are surrounded by cliffs and islands of beautiful red and black serpentine rock'. It was this description that gave her a destination for her impulsive escape, yanked here as if by a force from deep in the bowels of the earth.

Steep steps eroded into ancient cliffs snaked their way down towards the pristine beach. Her blonde hair, damp with morning mist, clung to the sides of her angular face as she negotiated the path. A waft of ozone teased her nostrils, encouraging her onwards. And then she was there. Kicking off stressed-out trainers, her toes curled and moulded into the firm sand leaving hardly an imprint as she took in the surroundings.

From nowhere she attempted a cartwheel before giggling and checking over her shoulder. 'Pathetic and ridiculous' his words spewed into her newfound idyll. Biting her lip and hissing out pain Annie turned a full circle and breathed in the magnificence of the beach sculptures glistening in greens and reds. Round the cove, caves called to her. From smooth caverns emerged tongues of indescribable beauty, scales of viridian and carnelian etched with ivory.

(Look what Dev's creative mind has done. Serpentine resembles snakeskin. Look at the snakelike vocabulary in her draft: moulted, glided, slithered, curled, moulded, hardly an imprint, angular face, and of course, tongue and snaked.)

Erratic (extract)
By Dev Jaffe

(Erratic – A rock or boulder that differs from the surrounding rock)

Horror of all horrors, there behind the rocks was the same individual who had commandeered Hattie's dining table the night before. First her table and now her rock, this was one intrusion too much. The man did not acknowledge her approach as she strode towards him but continued adding to his diagram. His note-making and sketching was punctuated with him leaning very close to the rock and inspecting it with a hand lens. This appeared pointless to Hattie as the rock looked the same all over.

'Move to the side', he ordered, 'you are making a shadow.'

Hattie did as commanded and said nothing. It did not seem odd that a complete stranger told her what to do. He was correct.

'Hold this', he ordered and gave her a tape measure. Several measurements later, he closed his notebook and headed to the next lump. 'We'll get three more done before the light goes if we hurry', in a way she found inexplicable, after all she had her own route to follow, they completed three more rocks.

'You were useful', he said and then as if prompted from deep inside 'Thank you'.

'What is the purpose of your activity?', she asked.

'I'm charting erratics', he replied, as if this explained things.

'Erratics?' Hattie questioned

'Rocks deposited when travelling ice sheets melted, they're different from the native rocks. They have a different history to the ones underneath.'

They trudged along in silence. At the hotel he told her to be at the table early and he would show her the paths the rocks had travelled.

He didn't greet her but opened his lap top and launched into detailed explanations. Supper they ate in silence. After the fruit salad and ice cream he stood up.

'We will do the lower slope tomorrow, 8.30 we leave.'

Better text Mum, she thought.

MUM CHANGE OF PLANS. TOMORROW I'M MEASURUNG ERRATICS AND WILL NOW STAY TILL SUNDAY

I love how she turned 'erratic' and 'serpentine' into fascinating characters. Think sideways. Turn that shrapnel into shells, fossils, rocks or characters. Make that egg cup work for you.

RESPONSES TO GAME 12

The Boy on the Beach image seems to work so well. Please feel free to share it – it is one of mine, so you don't need my permission. Just let me know, and a credit will do.

Here are some responses.

First, from Frances Hay, written at a Grist to the Mill session. She says, "*I remember scanning the photo, trying to get a sense of the landscape, and then my eyes zoomed in on the boy and his shadow. In that light, the boy can't see his shadow and I just got the idea of writing from the shadow's point of view. Then it really was like automatic writing, I just wrote furiously until you called time. It was such an inspiring exercise.*"

Unseen
by Frances Hay

He touches the shadow of my left hand with his own wet fingers, pressing down in the tidal mud, splaying out his fingers to finger each of mine. He's not looking at the rest of me extending out behind him on the surface of the shallow pool, quiet and unmoving here behind the sandbar and the loud, persistent waves.

I try to touch him, trace the yellowed callous on his tallest finger, push up against his wet palm. At this time of day, I lurk behind him. I cannot watch his face. He can't see my body, follow my gaze. I cannot meet his eyes. He's looking for something that's more interesting than me – perhaps small hermit crabs or shells of scallops who abandoned their houses long ago.

The waves advancing toward him don't attract him; nor do the oaks clinging to the cliff. I try to clasp his hand more tightly, but I am boneless, voiceless, the external part of him. I'm unable to pull him up to look him in our face.

Then we have a play, a monologue, from Jo Russ, working with me in that Grist to the Mill session.

A MOTHER'S STATEMENT
By Jo Russ

MOTHER: He was a good boy, mostly. There were the outbursts and, yes,the times he couldn't tell the truth but otherwise a good boy. This was where he felt good. Safe. He would wait for as long as it took for the tide to go out before searching for and choosing the largest, the '*best*' shallow pool after the tide had gone way out. Then with flat hands, fingers together, he would skim the water before digging both flat hands, like paddles, into the sand with its tiny little stones and bits of shell and then open his fingers and sieve the sand away until he found some treasure. The treasure was the seaglass he would sometimes find and bring to me in his little yellow bucket. "Found some more!" he'd cry out from the flat empty beach. He was so engrossed. There were other kids in the distance; curious heads bobbing, voices bouncing off high rocks above the bay. Far away from him and so different but that's the way he liked it. He just marvelled at the water as it washed over his hands ***(pause)*** washed them clean. Maybe he felt that he could filter out the sand and grit inside his head.

(Pause as she breathes in, looks out of the high window to her right and exhales. She looks down into her lap. Her hands are clutching tissues that she has inadvertently rolled into a ball. Tears well in her eyes and she clears her throat to continue)

That day I just couldn't get him to come in. I was reading my book and looking up every so often as I always did. I delivered his juice then a sandwich. There was no one else around; maybe a dog walker or two but other than that, just us. End of season. Digging for treasure.

(She smiles a brief, bright smile as she remembers the following anecdote)

Sometimes I would take an ice-cream cone down to him and it would mostly melt in one hand, held there over his head, completely forgotten with the ice-cream dripping down his hand. The seagulls would gather round but he was completely oblivious. Fish could have flown over his head and he wouldn't have noticed. Nothing could distract him from his 'magic sea pool'.

(Pause. She recalls him calling it this. The corners of her mouth lift slightly then turn down. She swiftly wipes her eye, swallows and continues)

It was getting quite late, and I had to get back to the shop. He never wanted to come so I gave myself extra time, you know, to allow for the delay in getting him to come. ***(pause).*** Now I wish I'd just dragged him but he would scream this high pitched scream as though someone had tried to break an arm or something. I was used to it but, well, I just couldn't touch him. Only talk to him. Persuade him ***(pause)*** or bribe him, like mums do, y'know.

The other kids in the distance had decided to come down. I couldn't see any parents, but I just thought they'd be on the other side of the rocks, y'know, while their kids went exploring. That's what we used to do; rock-pools and fishing for little crabs to put in our buckets. ***(pause).*** The kids wandered over to him and I thought, that's nice, even though I felt a bit nervous because they didn't know him. ***(pause).***

I checked the time and we had about ten minutes, so I left him to it. The other kids were watching him in his game, and it looked like they were joining in with the fanning of the hands and the raising of them until the water dripped through. I heard laughter. I heard his laughter, which was a rare thing. He was content, I think, but he wouldn't generally show it. Not the way other children can.

(She attempts to tell the next moment and stops. She snatches a sudden and sharp intake of breath and starts)

Then I heard it. I heard the scream and I saw that one of the kids, a bigger boy, had taken his spade. He would use it to make the pools deeper sometimes and it was always set to one side. It was an old one that belonged to his grandad. The other boy found it funny at first, that Max screamed like that. He held it above his head and swung it around. He threw it to his friends, and they all played catch with it while Max asked to give it back and jumped up to try and catch it. They didn't know, did they? How could they have known? I saw that it was all getting out of hand and even though the kids were just having fun, I could see that Max was very agitated by this point. I started to walk down, quickly, and then noticed that the boy stopped. He handed the spade back and turned with his friends to walk away. I watched them laughing and kicking up the sand. I called Max and started to walk back towards our things.

(Pause. She frowns and reprimands herself.)

I should have just grabbed him. I should have just…..but I didn't. I kept walking back thinking about the takings; there was £500 or more in that bag. I had saved enough time to take it to the bank. I checked and it was all there.

(Pause. She raises her hand to her forehead, closes her eyes and recalls in fractured detail)

Then there were different screams. Lots of voices; not just one. Then this heavy slap of a dead weight hitting the sand. Then I felt hot with terror and turned. I knew. I just knew.

(She becomes more agitated and desperate, re-living the event)

I ran as fast as I could. My feet were sinking, and I couldn't get to him. I couldn't stop him. The boy's arms were up and then they weren't. The others were screaming to stop, and I was telling them to stop screaming. *Please stop!!! Stop screaming!!!* One of them had a phone and called someone.

(She looks up and into the past)

That boy with all that energy and laughter and just having fun; wanting to play. Then all that life; fighting for it. Using all his strength to save it. The desperation and the pleading. I snatched the spade, but ....

(She stares, then smiles a weak smile and pleads)

Can I see him now? Can I see my boy?

And this, from the same Grist to the Mill session. A complete short story, again, inspired by the photo on page 13, and worked up after the session.

The Ridge
by Maria Sanger
Spring, 1831, Uig, Isle of Lewis

Mary runs barefoot along the shoreline in the rushing wind. Her red plaits fly behind her. She likes to race the sea mares as they ripple over the sand. Eventually, when the wind calms or she is out of breath she digs up sparkly pebbles that catch her eye and throws them into the sea. They skip across the surface and then disappear under the waves at a point where the greyish blue becomes greenish blue, the place known as the ridge. Papa often speaks of it, and Mary wishes he would swim out there with her, but he rarely goes to the beach. 'It's not for the likes of wee bairns,' he tells her.

Mary is almost eight years old, and she knows she can look after herself. Neither Ma nor Papa know that she understands the movements of the seabirds, that she can talk to the porpoises and the whales. But in the darkness of night, she hears Papa's voice. 'Mary, don't ever cross the ridge, or the kelpies will get you.'

Next morning Ma is digging for lug worms and collecting them in a bucket. Thin coils of sand give away each worm's hiding place. Mary's shadow twists and turns like the godwits on the shoreline. A thin layer of sea water rests on the sand, a remnant of the receding tide. She crouches down and stares at her reflection in this shimmering mirror of water, and her smock trails in the wetness.

Clouds shift overhead. Water ripples over ridges of golden sand and dark shapes gather. A strange sensation as though someone is watching her. She gazes at the cliffs and scans the dunes, but there doesn't seem to be anyone else here other than her and Ma. Below, waves spiral in shifting tones of greys and greens. Mary is transfixed by a dot that grows larger and larger. And now she sees it clearly. A boat rises in and out of the waves. Inside are rows of crowns. Bulging eyes gawp at her. A whole kingdom of crowns chorus with reedy voices, 'Come with us.' The image disappears.

The water sinks into the wet sand. She must have been leaning too heavily on it, for now there is a hole. Without thinking she slides her arm down deep into it. Something smooth brushes against her hand.

At the shoreline, she dips her toes into the water and the ridge calls out to her. She leaps forward into the swash towards the iridescent greens. Ma catches her and pulls her back. 'Mind yourself, Mary. A rogue wave will knock you under and then you'll be sorry.'

Mary holds her tongue. What did the boat mean? She counts the thistles in the dunes and watches the small flies burrowing into the sand. She picks up yellow crabs in the rock pools of the cove. They scurry towards the shoreline when she sets them down.

Clouds scud above; the gulls disappear in and out of the sea spray.

'We must go,' says Ma, dragging Mary away from the rocks.

'But why?', says Mary, pulling on her Ma's arm. Ma seems not to hear her but holds her head down against the squally wind. The laden bucket slows Ma's pace. Mary shudders, hoping her mother will not drop it. The sea tells her there is a boat coming. It is heading for the rocks. Her heart pounds with excitement.

'Heave Ho, hoist the sail.' The sailor's voice fades in a decrescendo. And then silence. The air chills her arms on the beach and she crouches in the darkness, but there is no sailor, just some planks of wood and bladderwrack. Nowhere to hide. The sands gleam under the haloed moon and the sea is smooth like ivory, yet always moving. She steps forward into the silvery light, and her boots crunch razor shells and dead crabs. She unties her pigtails and frees her thick hair. Something pokes out from the sand. She tries to pull it up, but it is heavy and stuck fast, gripped by the sand. The leather is strong in smell and has a large ivory buckle attached. Mary tears it from the bag and drops it into her pocket.

The sea sings and the waves ebb and flow, bringing figures from afar nearer and nearer to the shore. At first, they look like ships. Her gaze follows each one in on the tide, but they are not ships. They are horses on the sea. They slide through the foam onto the sand and fill her with a joy she has never known. They can be her friends. They are not only different in size to the pieces Papa plays with. Some have no face at all. But these knights are real. The horses thunder along the stretch of sand then rise up on their hooves before galloping back. She runs alongside them, but as her hair flies in her eyes she stumbles over some rocks and falls. Swerving, a knight reaches down, plucks her up into the air and suddenly, there she is perched, holding onto his armour. She hears the wolfish cries behind them. 'Berserkers,' shouts the Knight and he blows his trumpet in a rhythmic fanfare.

'The Warders, the Bishops, the Queens and the Kings,' he cries, and the figures process along the beach, dignified, their robes flowing behind them. They stop opposite Mary and for a moment their fixed stares unsettle her, but she manages a curtsey to the Kings and Queens, and they nod back. The warders and the pawns stand a way off by the rocks, by the wooden planks and bladderwrack and a body. They bow their heads in respect to the body.

'Come with us to the ridge,' say the chessmen, 'we can show you our kingdom and make you a red queen,' but Mary shakes her head, afraid to look at the body.

'Why not?' The White Queen's gravelly voice sounds as though sand fills her nose.

'The kelpies, the kelpies. Do you know who they are?' Papa's words come back to her.

'You will be safe with us,' they chorus.

'I have to get back home to Papa,' she says.

It is morning. Mary hears raised voices, and she puts her ear to the wall. A cluttering sound disturbs a crow that was sitting on the ridge of the back door. 'They've found a bundle,' it caws.

Ma is speaking. 'Thirty pounds for a bag of carved sprites. I can't believe that, Malcolm MacLeod.'

'Better to get thirty pounds for this bag of sprites than have to dig for lug worms or gather winkles for less than three shillings.'

'Keep your voice down. You'll wake the girl,' says Ma.

'We should at least show her,' says Papa, 'before I sell them to Roderick.'

'And put even more foolish ideas in that head of hers? 'Get rid of them, MacLeod, before she sees them.'

Mary hates it when they argue. In a moment, they'll be calling out for her. She hurriedly puts on the smock. The hemline is heavy with wet sand and salt. A wetness and scratchiness underfoot. Seaweed is stuck to her legs, and she can taste the salt on her mouth. She rummages in the drawer for some clean undergarments. In the pocket of her smock, she touches something smooth. It is still there. How she prised it from the bag! Bubbles of excitement rise up. For now, she puts the buckle safely back into the drawer, then closes the door behind her and clomps across the kitchen floor to the trestle.

'There you are, girl,' says Papa as she enters the kitchen. 'Look what I've found.' He drops the bag onto the table with a thud. Clumps of sand fall onto the trestle. He pulls out several crowned figures. She can see frayed stitches where the buckle was once attached.

'I'm not a child.' She pushes the bag away but cannot help staring at the bulging eyes. The little creatures are only as tall as her hand. 'I've seen them before.'

'Enough!' says Ma, spooning some eggs on a plate. She casts a strange glance at Papa. 'Such flights of fancy will get you in trouble, Mary.'

She knows the shrillness in Ma's voice. It always comes when her eyes narrow like that. 'But they spoke to me,' Mary says. 'They really did. And I saw a dead body on the beach.' Papa gives Ma a peculiar look and puts the chess pieces back in the bag quickly. Mary winces as Ma brushes her hair free of knots and plaits it tightly.

'Don't lie to your Ma,' says Papa. 'And promise me you'll keep away from the ridge. Now run along and help your Ma collect some winkles for supper.' He kisses the top of her forehead. Mary promises but crosses her fingers behind her.

The tide is turning, and Ma scoops the winkles from the rocks and drops them in a clean sack. Mary wanders off along the beach and finds a broken oar, half buried in the sand. 'Heave ho, hoist the sail,' she cries. Her feet march in time to the words and she relishes the sea spray on her face. Her toes scrape on the rock pools. She plucks out a crab, and now she is the knight on the horse running across the beach, with the oar trailing behind her. 'Not for the likes of wee bairns,' she scolds the crab.

'There you are, Mary. Put the oar down.' Ma's voice is weary, and she hobbles over, the sack filled with winkles. 'The waves will carry you off if you're not careful.'

Mary watches the gannets circle out at sea. If only she was free like them. She could go where she wanted.

'Let's go have supper and if you're good, I'll tell you a story,' says Ma.

'I don't want you to. Why can't Papa tell me a story?' Mary cries into the lashing wind.

'Papa has gone to Stornoway to sell the chess pieces,' sighs Ma. 'I told you he won't be home yet.'

Mary wants to know how he got the bag, but daren't ask.

It is nighttime. Mary takes the buckle from her drawer and holds it up to the light of the moon. 'The reedge; the reedge, come to the reedge,' it whispers.

She waits for Ma's gentle snores. Then creeps out of bed and out of the croft. Alone by the shoreline, she puts the buckle safely into the pocket of her pinafore and stoops to cup her hand in the lapping surf. It is icy and refreshes her forehead. She lifts her hand to the moon, eager to feel the breath of the tides on her skin. Dip your whole body into the waters, it tells her. Be brave. Cross the ridge.

'How will I know when I find it?'

'The sea will guide you,' says the moon. 'And I will guide the sea.'

Black horses swim towards Mary and encircle her. Your Papa is not coming home tonight, they say. 'You can stay here longer. You can play with us.'

'Why so glum? Come with us,' call the knights. 'Come and be a queen.'

Her arms and legs grow lighter as if they could float to the moon. The sand mirror gleams again in the moonlight and Mary looks into it. Her skin is so pale, and the pulse of her breath slows. The chessmen's' eyes mesmerise her. She hardly notices the kelp creeping over her toes and gently wrapping around her ankles, pulling her forward ever so slightly. Her feet disappear under the swirling spume, churned up by the kelpies that bob in the waves. Down she falls through misty vapours and burbling clouds. She does not need to breathe. 'Not for the likes of wee bairns.' Papa's voice breaks up. Gliding through the kelp canopies and forests she descends to the lower weed plains. Jellyfish swim past as her body floats through the gaping mouth of caves, the labyrinth of the drowned. Seaweed flutters in her face. Out from her pocket falls the buckle. Down, down deep on the seabed floor, Mary sinks and joins the rows of sleeping chessmen.

The Lewis Chessmen were found on a beach in Uig in 1831. The exact whereabouts of their discovery is unknown. There are several accounts as to what happened to the pieces immediately after their discovery. Malcolm Macleod sold most of the Lewis chessmen, through Roderick Ryrie (or Pyrie or Ririe), a merchant from Stornaway, to a man called Forrest in Edinburgh for £30. (Stratford, N., 1997. The Lewis Chessmen and the enigma of the hoard. London: British Museum.)

RESPONSE TO GAME 14

This also comes from Grist to the Mill, when we were listening to Arvo Part's *Spiegl im Spiegl.*

Maria Sanger wrote a bank of words, prompted first by Beauty.

beauty silver water willows swallows clouds
serene floating trees arms heads bells flowers shimmering
people reflections dip dangling riverbanks

Then, from these words she wrote her first poem.

The willows dangle arms
Trailing in the shimmering water
Reflecting wispy strands of cirrus
Flowers hanging heads in respect
As the flax bends at the water's edge
Kingfishers dip and dive
Lovers rolling on the banks
Watch the tumbleweed drift.

Maria says: "*It was interesting to see how this panned out as I hadn't written any poetry before. Some of the words from the word bank felt more immediate than others.*"

RESPONSE TO GAME 18

This, from Ali McGrane

She says: "*The first draft was created in your workshop at the Flash Fiction Festival, 2019. You talked about getting inside someone's skin to see the world through their eyes, and the prompt was literally that – finding a different skin and putting it on. My brain went to bees.*"

Many rests and edits later, it was published in The Flash Flood 2021 http://flashfloodjournal.blogspot.com/2021/06/i-find-bee-skin-hanging-behind-bathroom.html and nominated for Best Small Fictions and Best of the Net.

I Find the Bee Skin Hanging Behind the Bathroom Door
By Ali McGrane

It slips on easily. My body flows into the shape as though bee DNA lurked there all along. Snug in the legs and a tickle where the sting is lodged.

Vision zooms and mosaics. My wings open of their own accord, roll and lift like paddling oars. I rise above gigantic objects I barely recognise as my own mess.

Buzz overtakes me. I am buzz incarnate, drawn to the siren call. I zig and zag, crash and slide, fooled again and again by the window's lure.

Believing the lie at last, I dodge your trapping hands, your simple eyes still blind to my shifting form, and tumble a dusted sunbeam through the opening door. Out into honeyed air.

Patterning bodies fold me in, and the dance is joy and gluttony and sway. Tongue-smell, jaw-taste, wing-breath, flooding. Thighs pollen thick. Sweetness and urging. Flight.

RESPONSES TO GAME 19

Someone in the house.

First, a thought-provoking meta-fiction response from Tim Love, who came to a workshop at the Flash Fiction Festival.

> ***A promising writer***
> ***by Tim Love***
>
> Here, you'll find no action-packed start followed by info-dumping. Nobody will die – after Covid and the Ukraine, we've had enough of all that. The protagonist won't be a struggling writer. And it won't all be a dream.
>
> If it was long ago, the person wouldn't be masked, but it's the Covid years, so I can't see who's coming down my loft ladder. If it was long ago, the dress would mean it's a woman, but I can see he's very much a man underneath. Being a modern story, I should have started it by saying that my mobile's flat so I can't call 999. As I reach for my journal to scribble notes, he sees me.
>
> "Are you a Ukrainian squatter?" I ask.
>
> "No. Only a transvestite. I was in my loft with my mask mending the asbestos partition when I saw through a hole your chest of costumes. There's a party tonight and I had nothing nice to wear. I couldn't resist."
>
> "It's my mother's. She was an actress. At least, that's what she said. I never knew my father. Maybe they're his pantomime outfits."
>
> "Why don't you come with me then? You could get loads of material for your stories," he says nodding at my empty journal. "Looks like you need all the help you can get."
>
> I haven't said whether I'm male or female, straight or gay, old or young. It doesn't matter to him. To be honest, I don't know

what I am any more – I've written too many stories. I roll my wheelchair towards him. "Thanks. I'd like that," I reply. "So how do cripples like you get up in the loft?" he asks. "What loft?" I say and he disappears into another story leaving me feeling guilty for dreaming yet again.

Maria Sanger from Grist to the Mill also sent this:

First, she wrote down atmosphere words, to help her create.

A sense of the solitary, isolated, alone, musty.

She then considered the questions:

Who is this?
Where are they living?
What clues are they leaving?
Why are they there?
Is this benign?
How are they discovered? Or are they?

She says: "*My response slightly deviated as I was writing. The place was a caravan in which the protagonist, waiting for her partner to return from a walk, has inadvertently entered the wrong caravan. They haven't been there for some months. The caravan belongs to the man with the cap with the dog. As I wrote on, the situation became more hostile. By using winklepickers, I wanted to set the story a little back in time.*"

Untitled
by Maria Sanger

My heels slipped on the damp, squelchy floor and I landed on my knees in a wet patch. I knew I should have worn sensible shoes. I could still hear Leonard's voice reprimanding me. I stood up, dusted off the red rust particles that had stuck to my legs. My immediate thought was that it had been a leak, but the ceiling, although tarred with smoke, was dry.

The paint on the door hadn't been peeling this badly last time we were here. Still last winter had been a rough one. But what was that smell? Where was Leonard?

Perhaps he had already been in with the milk while I was out. That'd be it. We had always managed to bring the bad Devon weather with us and indeed on every trip we'd ever been on. I could do with a cuppa. I pulled at the fridge handle, but it would not budge. By the third attempt it gave way, but the fridge was almost empty except for ugh...a dark yellow liquid in a glass. I slammed the door shut not wanting to know what it might be. Surely, he would be here soon. It was not like him to be this long. Outside, the caravan park looked bleak – a miry field – it was late in the season and most caravanners had upped and gone home. I could have sworn there'd been another caravan next to us when I arrived earlier.

I hadn't wanted to go for a walk across the cliffs, not in these winklepickers, but he had insisted he would, so instead, I ventured to the next field to pick some blackberries. Even in early October, these blackberries were late. Never pick blackberries after 30 September, Leonard had told me often. It'll bring bad luck. They were delicious and I still had the juice stains on my palm.

Outside the caravan, a broad fella was walking across the field with a dog. His dark cap was pulled down over his forehead and he was pulling on the dog's lead and shouting at the poor creature. I thought I saw him glimpse this way, so I hid away from the tattered net curtains. There was something strange about him and I didn't like the way he treated his dog. Its head and tail were so forlorn. My nerves jangled – what had got into me today? Surely Leonard would be back soon.

The smell was growing stronger. A mix of turpentine or metallic, or something else. I couldn't work it out. Wherever was Leonard?

And then I pushed open the bedroom door. Under the window, an old mattress had been pulled up on its side and flocks of material had been eaten through. Some of the stuffing was all over the floor. Must have been rats or mice, I supposed. In the middle of the small area, charred sticks had been piled high, and there were remnants of bones – some looked like chicken – others larger that I didn't recognise. There was some blood on the floor and when I looked closer there were blotches on the mattress. It didn't seem like anyone could have stayed here for months. The place needed a thoroughly good clean. I heard footsteps and a scuffling sound outside.

'Leonard! Is that you?' I jumped to my feet, awash with relief that he was back.

The handle turned and the door opened.

The dog growled and the broad fella with the cap stood in the door frame. He edged towards me and I could see there was no room for me to push past. His eyes were colourless and he began to laugh.

RESPONSE TO GAME 23

This was written during a Grist to the Mill session, after we read poet Dean Atta's wonderful version of 'I come from'.

I Come From
by Rosie Mowatt

I come from home-made white sauce on cauliflower dressed in Sunday best
And ivory handled knives and forks side by side on the dining room table
I come from home-brewed elderflower champagne, hidden in my brother's wardrobe.

I come from sea salted air, frost forming on the inside of our bedroom window,
Breathing out to warm frozen fingers. I come from getting dressed in front of three
Electric bars, holding our skirts and knitted tights to the heat.

I come from riding on the back of mum's bicycle and being handed to the bus
conductor, a label around my neck, please put this child off at the lake grounds.
I come from Fry's five creme bars on a Saturday and sticky chocolate fingers.

I come from singing in the school choir and walking to church in a crocodile
of paired up children. I come from learning to swim on a pebble beach walking
a mile across mud flats to the edge of the water lapping at my universe.

RESPONSE TO GAME 28

This, from Rosie Mowatt, again, working in a Grist to the Mill session: She says: "*We had to imagine a place we wouldn't want to be and a creature that we would want to be. My places: A place you would not want to be: Birmingham bullring, city centre. A creature you'd like to be: An otter.*"

Cheesecake Economics
by Rosie Mowatt

At freshers, I catch a glimpse of my otterly coils
reflected violet in your beady eye,
staring enraptured. You, coyly convinced
I won't notice your unblinking gaze.

Landlubber locked, we're on the run. Our paws
entwined, we blubber down Corporation Street,
ignoring the cries of straight American dudes
peddling their transcendental dreams.

Slipping, sliding through swivel doors
to sanctuary. In Rackhams, we point silky noses
towards patisserie, whiskers twitching, pink tongues
lolling for cheesecake – one pound a slice.

We make a bullring picnic set in concrete,
cheesecake nibbled on grass scrubland
encircled by juggernauts spiralling upwards
to fly in the eye of spaghetti junction.

Our first year out in the wild, we opt
for life lessons. We save up student pounds,
skip lectures and study the economics
of cheesecake – one slice at a time.

RESPONSES TO GAME 33

This, from David Lloyd, working with me at an Arvon week, at the lovely Lumb Bank.

His two folded slips of paper said:

1. Undertaker

2. Picking all the blue flowers in the park

Flowers for Emily
by David Lloyd

Gwynfor feels exhausted. He sits in the undertaker's office and inhales the embalming fluid that's drifted in from the mortuary next door. Eight back-to-back funerals have left him feeling like there's no beauty left in the world.

Two of the services were for young people, sixth formers, celebrating A-level grades; both killed in the same automobile crash.

It's a small town. He knew both of them and remembers the girl's mother as Westlife's "I'll see you again" played over the crematorium's PA system.

His eyes start to well up; hay fever triggered by lilies which crowned a clutch of coffins. He looks at the calendar knowing his vacation is still three months away. He yearns for those days by the lake where he grew up close to Snowdonia. The landscape and the smell of pines on the forest floor will restore him as watches wildlife capturing their movement with his camera. As he drifts off in his chair he starts to sneeze repeatedly. He struggles to breathe and reaches for his inhaler shoved in the back of his top desk drawer.

As the clock chimes 7pm he remembers it's his partner's birthday and he's forgotten to buy a present. He locks up and walks towards the park as the sun begins to adopt a tangerine hue.

The gates are chained. He clambers over railings, lands awkwardly, clutches his ankle and staggers forward. Gwynfor starts to pick all the bluebells he can lay his hands on. He carries them gently, lays them down on the grass, creates a bouquet and the world changes. Afterwards as he walks home, he sneezes and sneezes.

His eyes fill with tears.

And another, from a Grist to the Mill session:

The two folded slips of paper read:

1. Knight of the Thimble

2. Grape Dryer

The writer said: "T*he response became slightly more surreal than I expected!*"

Knight of the Thimble
by Maria Sanger

Halt, who goes there?
He is the thimble keeper, the knight who keeps watch in the long nights.

The Knight is tall, a lean man with long fingers that daintily stretch out. On the end of each finger sits a porcelain thimble. Beware those clunky bells sitting on his thumbs don't hurt your knuckles. You're admiring them, I can tell, but let me warn you against it. Mademoiselle's voice is rather grating when she speaks, don't you agree? She too has her favourites. In the mirror she watches you.

The Knight guards each thimble with a fierceness that we all think is eccentric for just a tailor who once made suits. I wish I had never met him. I often think back to those early days he used to cut out the patterns for us ladies-in-waiting and altered our dresses to keep up with the fashions. Once he was modest but has since become ever more controlling and pig-headed. Many outside our circle do not know that he is the Knight of the Thimble who protects the noble King's collection for three hundred and sixty-five days. And he won't hear of being confused with the Knight of the Templar, whose fighting hands are neither so white nor so smooth. Nor will he be called a Teutonic Knight who helps with the sick, which is, in my view, a far more commendable pursuit. But our Knight will not tolerate blood on his hands. He is clear about that, for he hates the thought of staining any of our white delicate porcelain. I warn you to leave while you have the opportunity, for it often happens so quickly. How are you to know that each thimble casts its spell and then you will be sucked into our existence. Who could not fail to be moved by a pretty face? Or a beautiful garden, and then that lingering becomes hours, days, years. You wake up, basking in dappled light of the russet browns and yellows of the porcelain autumnal grapevine you were so admiring, and then you lose count of how many times you have witnessed it. Or perhaps instead you linger on the frosty silence of the snowflakes and Mademoiselle's chilled recommendations cast their effect on you. Once I too breathed the words of life and even spoke to The Knight of the Thimble while she watched me in the mirror. And She cast me in porcelain. As you can see, Apollo sits on my right side; on the opposite side is Pan. Naively, we all thought there is such a thing as choice, but now I share time between the summer gardens of Versailles or the Medici gardens in Florence. True, my fate could be worse. I might be sleeping with the Pig-Headed Knight of the Thimble. Watch me weave in and out of the orange trees of Versailles. On my left, Hephaestus forges creations of fire and bronze and makes my ears ring as he hammers against it. No, I wouldn't recommend it. Leave while you can. Over there sits Chaos, whose gaping mouth is taciturn. The badger-like eyes of the Knight of the Thimble are watching Mademoiselle. She of the Thimble always crosses his thoughts, but no, perhaps I am mistaken. I do believe he is rather taken by you. Mademoiselle is undoubtedly sculpted with the most eloquent curves, you understand, but your youthful energy keeps him preoccupied. Yes, go on, lead him on if you dare! Provoke her! He flatters you! Go on, stroke his face with your long scarlet fingernails. Oh, he is confused, the toad! But see Mademoiselle scowls at you in the mirror and shakes her fists. Oh, what joy. Let fury come to the fore! She is under no illusion, and by what illusions will she be shattered? The mirror cracks. Porcelain crunches. Bells clink. No more thimbles. We stand in the shells of porcelain, and I look in the cracks of the red flecked mirror. I step over Mademoiselle's body and compare my long red fingernails with his gritty, nail-bitten ends.

RESPONSE TO GAME 35

A memory – switched Oulipo-fashion
by Maria Sanger

Oulipo – Without an I

You stroked the butterfly carefully, the antennae brushed on your palm. You laughed; your hand powdered with fae dust. Red, purple, black-streaked plumage emerged from the pupa. Tell me, creature, you say, where shall you fly? Up and over the butterfly bush.

Oulipo – Without an O

I lift the butterfly carefully, its antennae brushing against my palm. It tickles my skin. Red, purple, black, streaky, veined wings that bristle with excitement. Its antennae twitch then she flies away high up in the buddleia bush.

Then taking the above ideas and melding into one:

On the lower slopes of Olympus, the falls roar behind us and the freshness of the spray cools my skin. I cup Apollo in my hands, and he tickles my palm with the softest of white feathers. I slowly let the afternoon light in, and he bristles with excitement. 'Tell me Apollo, where will you fly? His red eyes stare back, and his translucent wings briefly flicker and then he soars through the forest dipping and darting for nectar, here and there, further and further into the distance, a glimmer, a speck and then gone.

RESPONSE TO GAME 36

From a Grist to the Mill session.

Fruity
by Rosie Mowatt

'Hurry, we haven't got much time.'

I could hear the urgency in his tone, as I struggled to keep up with him in the dark corridor. It smelt musty down here in the basement, a forgotten and unused part of the old people's home, or At Sun's Set, as the glossy brochure liked to call it.

I'd brought along a walking stick for balance, and it took extra effort to place it carefully in front of me, without a telltale thump to give away our whereabouts. We'd decided the best time would be the start of Eastenders – any noise of the shifting basement door would be covered by the duff, duff, duff of the opening theme tune. That meant we had exactly twenty-seven minutes to make it to our secret stash and back to our seats again.

'Right, I'm here at the doorway – you ready?'

I don't know when Arthur became such a close ally. It was true what they said, though – thick as thieves when there's a bit of mischief involved. And we did enjoy the subterfuge of it all. The way we'd shifted hundreds of tins of fruit over the months from the kitchen pantries and stashed them in this forgotten corner.

Arty flared a cigarette lighter and we were suddenly lit up, our shadows thrown distorted on the corridor walls. The light glinted on the silver of the rows and rows of tins piled up on the shelves in the cupboard in front of him. He reached in and grabbed one from each of the two shelves.

'We want a mix, don't we, Doll?' he said, passing them back to me to stash in my cardigan pockets. 'Bottom one's peaches, top one's pears, that'll do.'

We smiled serenely to nurse Maggie as she switched on the lights at the end of the programme. 'Enjoy that, did we?'

'Must have dropped off, to be fair, might have to catch up again on iPlayer!' Arty winked at me.

'Yeah, me, too – time for bed, I think', as we disappeared to our rooms for a midnight feast at 9pm of fruit salad eaten straight from the tin.

RESPONSES TO GAME 37

This response comes from Wendy Ogden, a writer I swap ideas with now and again. She collided my writing game with a list of words from her writing group (see, I said lists of random words were a good idea!) And she is honest about the time she took battling this story out.

She says: *My first thought when I read Vanessa's prompt was that a house with no front wall was in danger of falling down. That seemed like an interesting scenario to start with but then I had to decide which house, or what type. I had a list of words from my weekly writing group and it seemed very lucky that together the prompts could answer the who, what, where, when and why questions, or some. Useful questions if you're stuck. The words I had to play with were: countryside, barn, pigs, fog, and coronation. So it looked like I had me a farmhouse.*

The image of the missing wall gave me an open house situation with people arriving to see it, so I created a married couple on a day out in the countryside for a viewing. All I had to do then was write the house down, and I had a lot of fun doing that. The story I expected to be a flash turned out to be the longest short I have written. The characters stepped up, or went up the stairs, and took over the story.

It has occurred to me that the above two paragraphs make the process look easy. It really wasn't and it took two weeks to get a first draft. Other peoples houses and lives are so interesting though. Thanks to Vanessa for sharing the exercise with me.

Untitled (extract)
by Wendy Ogden

We were all looking at the open front house, like a crowd might admire a graffiti picture on a blank wall, but I felt like a miniature child looking up at a giant dolls house. Like beach people watching a passing fishing boat, our eyes all followed the pigs, wandering out of the living room, through the hall, past the stairs, and into the next one. This was a dining room. We all shuffled along to the left to see what the pigs got up to next. They snuffled around the table mainly, must have been hungry poor things and the pickings looked slim.

The table had a bright yellow gingham cloth on, like a little spot of sunshine on a cloudy day. One of the chairs was pulled back from the table and there was the remains of a meal left there, presumably the previous night's supper. It was like a child had just messed around with the food, pretending to eat it, and then left the table in a strop. A man with binoculars identified mould growing on brown lumps. We all jumped when a chicken, disguised as an ornament, jumped down from a sideboard onto the table and started pecking at a slice of stale bread and butter. None of the pigs reacted.

'That's farmers for you,' Alan said. 'He's removed every brick, pane and window from the house, and tidied them all away neatly somewhere, but couldn't be bothered to clear his dinner.'

'How do you know the farmer was a man?' Blondie responded, still clutching onto the arms of two random men.

She made a fair point, but by now most of us were looking around. I think it only occurred to us all then, that no building materials were stacked, or laying, in front of the house or anywhere around the yard. We all looked around for bricks, windows, the door, or dust even, but it was as if they had never existed.

And this is from a very new writer, who joined us on the Grist to the Mill evenings only recently. She says: '*I wrote it by hand and transcribed it. I haven't edited it at all. I hope it's not too boring but what I will say is that the exercise was an invaluable one for me because I didn't think I could write on demand. You have given me a quiet confidence to carry on and just write freely.*'

The Wrecked House
By Sophia Skyers

It was a dark cloudy day. The rain had begun to fall, the fine kind of rain that soaks through to the bones quickly. The bulldozer had been in earlier, in the week it was the decanting and now demolition. The entire façade of a row of three terraces had been demolished, the roof decapitated, leaving only the back wall intact. The area was surrounded by the entrails of the lives of its former inhabitants, flytipping of old matresses, clothes, terry nappies, nylon sheets, old newspapers mixed with sludge.

Inside, the remnants of sad lives, a bent and twisted beer can, cigarette stubbs, a battered settee splling its inards. Looking up at the grey clouds shrouding the building above, what lives? What history those walls to tell.

RESPONSE TO GAME 39

Such surprising responses came from Electra Rhodes's tweet. Here's one I loved, from a Grist to the Mill session, again.

> ***Letting go***
> ***by Rosie Mowatt***
>
> When the RSPCA arrived to clear out the newts, you'd already left for work that day. You missed the drama of scooping them into buckets of water with a large, netted sieve, seeing their wriggling bodies slip and slither along the transparent sides. They reminded me of large slugs trying to slither up the side of the bath. They reminded me of you.
>
> I missed the newts more than I would have guessed. Those first few days after they'd gone, I crept down to the basement to see whether any of their kin had found their way back up the drainpipe, but there was an eerie silence where they once had been.
>
> I was glad I still had the dreams to explore. I mixed them up with a pinch of weather in the large iron cauldron and submerged them in boiling water from the kettle. I thought I heard a sharp hiss. The sudden heat made my eyes sting, steam swirling around and above my head as images of you with her spun like a tornado around the room. Funny how I still miss the newts more than you.

RESPONSES TO GAME 41

Here's a response from Julie Reid, who worked with me at Gladstone's Library:

She says: "*I found this exercise phenomenal! It helped me to sharpen my observation skills.*"

'A place where you were happy...'
by Julie Reid

Battersea Park, London. The first large expanse of greenery I had ever seen; it was a huge contrast to the streets where I lived. On the street it was crowded, overly filled up with flats piled on top of each other. The Park provided an area – a vast area – within which I felt space enough to grow. The Park became my go to place for solitude.

The Park became my place, my refuge. I called it my garden, and that made perfect sense to me – a child without space to call her own acquired an open space within which she could walk for miles, run, do whatever she wanted within reason.

The tall trees made me feel protected in some way. The weeping willow was a container for my tears. The numerous other trees – not too sure of names – greeted me, were friends to me, silent custodians of my park, my space.

I remember the bowling green – pristine, neat, tidy. Then there was the aviary – a cornucopia of different species of birds. There was the open-air paddling pool, the adventure playground, and the ordinary playground – well that's what I called it, as it contained the equipment that I most associated with a playground: a climbing frame, swings, a seesaw, merry go round – all the things that kept youngsters occupied for hours.

And yes, I spent hours in this place, hours creating a home from home, my space. Oh, I forgot – the boating lake… the fun fair, the mound, the path, the athletics track, the pond, the ducks.

And another - a change of timbre from the Petersfield Museum course.

'A place where you were unhappy'
by Jane Dunster

The Sixth Form Centre

Positively Scandinavian, I suppose. Wood cladding, clean straight lines, with a hatch into the kitchen (tea, coffee, disputes about the washing up rota). A record player blares out Depeche Mode, or possibly the soundtrack to Grease. There is one wall completely covered with notices, and two small classrooms for Economics and Business Studies.

If you are leaving school for any reason there is a sign out sheet on the notice board. I walk a lot at lunchtimes. I wander into town, past the cemetery where a woman was killed - the son of the bus driver who takes me into school has been imprisoned for this, in what is later ruled a miscarriage of justice.

I am unhappy. Perhaps I am not loved. I remember one day Glen hugging me because my eyes streamed with tears. I was trying out contact lenses. But though I do not usually cry, I am unhappy most of the time. School has been a safe place but the room is not safe because even friends are cruel.

This is where I hit Sarah. She did not care, not at all. I slapped her and ran to the changing rooms and hid. School did not blame me. Somehow they saw what I was, though I did not know. I was an unhappy child without an unhappy childhood. I spent a deal of time escaping. I haunted abandoned classrooms. I hung round the History Department until sent away. I read books no-one had read in ages: Lucy Fitch Perkins' Twins books, Proust in white, blue and yellow covers, The Forsyte Saga. Anything long enough to be absorbed into.

I'm not sure what the others were doing. I couldn't connect with them. Their experience was not mine. Work was safer.

I remember the night the *alternative* alternative school band Pubic Hare were playing. The Head of Sixth Form, Mr Reid: 'Dont, please don't...Oh well, if you really must...' followed by the inevitable dropping of trousers. I fear I am Mr Reid sometimes, as a parent and at work.

Turning ever inwards. What is 'a loner'? I sat on the steps in the wind. I went to classes that were not mine. I was to be A Great Advocate - of what?

Years later, my teenage child was found in the gym, overwhelmed and anxious. We are sometimes unhappy, but we do not lead unhappy lives.

RESPONSE TO GAME 45

This comes from a Grist to the Mill evening.

'Left': meaning both 'departed' or 'remained behind'.

Swept up
By Rosie Mowatt

He should have listened to mother but they'd had a huge row.

'You can't marry your cleaning lady! The wrong one's worse than no-one – you'll see.'

'You're just jealous. Ever since Dad died and you were left on your own.'

He was so certain that he'd make mother see, but the fragrant nuptial air was soon overwhelmed by a pungent chemical stench. On Thursdays, he became another stain to be bleached.

He opened the dishwasher mid-cycle. Peering over the top of his steamed-up glasses, he sighed. Each slot of the cutlery basket was filled with a pair of lacy panties. One pair had risen on the tide, taunting him. Caught on the central spray arm, its elastic had unravelled with each spin, fraying at the edge, allure rinsed. He glanced up at the ceiling.

He traced her progress overhead as she lunged into the corners of bedrooms, spiders spinning as she sucked them up still shrouded in web. He imagined the dust motes shivering in sun beams, seeking shelter. A place to rest.

Disturbed, he pulled a shrunken jumper over the scorched sleeve of his freshly laundered shirt. He counted out £20 in cash and left it on the kitchen table. Only a few months ago, the simple transaction had been enough. The door rattled as he left, drowned out by the droning vacuum.

RESPONSE TO GAME 48

This writer, Caro Johnson, working with me at Petersfield Museum, collided memory and imagination in this response:

Finding something underwater
by Caro Johnson

Last time we were here it had been raining, raining, raining and the water was high. Too high for paddling, too high for exploration, it covered the stones in the yard and filled the dip in the road outside; Uncle Jeremy had to put on the waders and help to push the cars of unwary drivers out of the flood.

This time it's summer and the water has gone down and confined itself to where it should be. We pick our way barefoot over the stones, past the brick-built dog kennel and into the stream. The first step is icy in spite of the sun. The water is always flowing, moving, never still long enough to be warmed. We have the grassy banks on either side and I know that beyond the righthand bank is the road, going the same way that we are. We duck under the bridge that carries the path from the garden gate that nobody uses to the door into the house that nobody uses.

The banks become muddier, clay-like. I wonder if we could use it for pottery. We turn away from the road. We're nearly up to our knees now, mud squidging between our toes. And ahead, through the water, a gleam of silver. I see it first, a glint where the sun and water meet. For a moment neither of us moves. Somewhere a magpie calls out.

RESPONSE TO GAME 49

This lyrical piece is from Martyn Sands, working with me at Petersfield Museum on the Just Write course.

He says: "*After this suggestion, I spent a while on Google, and got really into the science of the Northern Lights, and the photos…I penned to say, I really don't usually write like this!*"

Northern Lights
by Martyn Sands

Only in the silence of a still mind can we start to tune in to the cosmic transmission, projected through time and space only to dance above us in a magnetic performance of flowing emerald and crimson waves.

A distant message of oneness chatters through the static as we close our eyes and gently turn the dial, searching for the perfect time to stop. In the here and now we are immersed in the majestic transitory nature of our experience.

It's time to dance with the light.

RESPONSE TO GAME 50

Some wonderful surreal definitions follow - thanks to Alice Wakefield for her notes from our week at Gladstone's Library.

Please feel free, as well as making your own surreal definitions, to dip into this list to inspire new 'things'...

A SHIP is a privilege not afforded to everyone a second time around. The first time will be a blessing, or a blemish enhanced or deprived of love.

A VIOLIN is too big and of mournful events, best forgotten.

A MAP is an iceberg smothered in glorious glitter.

A SNAKE is something that shows you the truth. But drop it, and it breaks – if that happens, it's bad luck for seven years.

A MOTHER is something you can float on. However, when it's in spate, it is dangerous – best steer clear.

A LILY is dangerously beautiful, alert and lithe in hunting.

SNOW is an ethereal being created by fire to obscure the edges of fear.

A DOOR is a dream of magical enchantment.

A CLOWN is a thing of joy until it goes wrong. Then it is an accursed field sent to torment us.

A STORM is where I feel cosy, safe, inspired by my books and records, which are as family as my family is to me (but with fewer hugs).

A COMPUTER is warmth in times of shrivelling need, a curse in parched times of hunger.

A CASTLE is a challenge to the feeble knees of the elderly and a delight to gazelles and youngsters, especially in summer.

A MIRROR is often bizarre, sometimes rebellious, but usually a safe place to travel.

A RIVER is a barrier to the infinite sum of possibilities we want to explore but are afraid to explore.

A HOME is a many splendid thing to live in.

A NIGHTINGALE is metallic, historic sometimes, beautfiul, dramatic and awfully dangerous.

A TIGER is cold, slimy and long. Never trust one with your kids.

SMOKE is a white sheet that goes wooo-ooo in the night.

A SWORD is a crash of wind, rain, thunder, a torrent of rain falling from the sky, peppered with hail or snow shaking the earth.

THE SUN is inconvenient when it blocks the lane and prevents you from getting out, but it's very pretty, especially when its sparkly, but its ugly when it melts.

A STORY is a template for an interesting voyage of adventures.

MY THINKING is a constant companion giving nourishing food to the ears of the soul.

A GHOST is a concealer of melancholy, a bright face fronting the tears within a deceiver of children.

A HILL is a healing birdlike worm, a pioneer who barred the pains and horrors of war and silenced their camp in the darkness so that beauty could be seen, and her soul healed.

RESPONSE TO GAME 51

This is from Julie Reid, who worked with me on a residential course at at Gladstone's Library. I gave out a choice of postcards and photos. Julie chose the stained-glass artwork.

She says: "*This was an exercise where we chose a picture – it could have been a picture of a character, a setting or something miscellaneous and we could choose one or as many as we wanted. I chose a wonderful picture that was a swirl of purple and blues. The image reminded me of an angel. As a result, I wrote the start of a short story called 'The Metal Angel. It's about a young boy, the only survivor of a bomb in his community in the desert, perhaps in Afghanistan or another contemporary war zone.*"

The Metal Angel
by Julie Reid

Faisal's alone again. There's no time for thoughts, just actions. He needs to go before night fall; desert temperatures drop so drastically. His life may be in more extreme danger from that shift in climate than from his captors. He notices the abandoned jeep – the rebel soldiers dead, laid out almost orderly on the ground. The minute grains of sand get in his eyes, which overfill with moisture as he wipes his face. Either he moves now or never. The engine's still running, the doors askance. He's in the seat before he realises he doesn't understand the language of the vehicle. He's seen jeeps move, but he's never driven one. But there's no time, no options, he has to move. Fast. Pulling the door to, his right-hand rests on the steering wheel. Mumbling a prayer – he thinks of the Angel Gibrel – a protector roaming the skies, even these skies where drones, aircraft and numerous bad things reside, and puts his food on the pedal. The jeep lunges forward. He takes his foot off the pedal and tries the adjoining one. The jeep stops. That's all he needs to know – he has communication with the thing that will take him away from imminent danger. In fits and starts, his new redeemer transports him into the desert. He sees no-one and feels relief for the first time, allowing himself a faint smirk. Gibrel heard his prayer. He doesn't know how long his metal angel is in motion, he has no idea how far removed he is from his captors. The jeep stops. He hits the steering wheel, pushes the pedals – first with his right foot, then his left food, then he gets off the seat, crunches down between the steering wheel and the pedals and moves them with his hands. He hits them – frantically screaming at their lack of animation, their cold indifference to his need to move.

RESPONSE TO GAME 51 and a half

Sarah Oakes is a visually impaired writer who wrote with me at the Flash Fiction festival.

She says: "*It was quite freeing to let rip and get this off my chest, putting my frustrations on paper. I know that none of the things mentioned will change (although the sight loss charity I work for and RNIB are working on campaigns) or listen to what I need to make changes. So, it was nice to rant about it somewhere as sometimes, stories are the only places the world hears you.*"

An Open Door
by Sarah Oates

Reading is an open door, a portal to a world of words and wonder. Please don't shut it on me. But with printed text, that's what you do. And I struggle to open that door. Magnifier skidding across pages to keep up and ending up exhausted halfway.

But with Audible, that door swings wide open. The world of words welcomes me, invites me, accepts me. Stories dance in my ear, no need to struggle. And I can experience it more intimately, part of the narrative too. I wish more people would see, would keep the door open, but they don't.

AFTERWORD

I hope you have an interesting time with these games and that they open up some good 'somethings' for you.

I also hope that you can see how *everything* can become inspiration for writing. Whether it is a newspaper article, a photograph, a website stumbled across on Google, a piece of music, even the back of a loo door at St Pancras.

If I've given you ideas to make your own writing games, then yippee! All these games are based on things I notice that seem to open up ideas. Writers sometimes say, apologetically, 'I'm afraid I changed the house in your game to a shed. Or France to Spain. Or a mountain to a lake.' To which my answer has to be:

'I'm so glad! You made it yours. Enjoy.'

There's no magic here, just observation, and inspiration from other writers and teachers too. And a bit of creativity. The real magic happens in the hands of those writers who engage with games like this, who bring their unique take on the world to the page.

Teachers and facilitators like me, we are the lucky ones, helping the emergence of new writing.

RESOURCES

A few more resources I find great for opening up my own writing and giving me all kinds of ideas for teaching too:

Finding Your Writer's Voice, by Thaisa Frank and Dorothy Wall

Inside Fictional Minds, by Dr Stephany Carty

The Five-Minute Writer, by Margaret Geraghty

More Five-Minute Writing, by Margaret Geraghty

The Penguin Book of Oulipo

What If, by Anne Bernays and Pamela Painter

A Swim in a Pond in the Rain, by George Saunders

On Poetry, by Jackie Wills

Writing Poems, by Peter Sansom

642 things to write about, by the San Francisco Writers' Grotto

plus

Google

Wikipedia

The news

Music

Twitter

Photos

The world in general

plus

Books - everything. Poetry, flashes, stories both long and short, fiction, non fiction.

Books mentioned herein:

Randall Jarrell's Book of Stories New York Review of Books, 1958.

The Lost Pianos of Siberia by Sophy Robers. Doubleday 2020

ACKNOWLEDGEMENTS

Thank you so much to:

All those generous writers from my workshops who have offered their often unedited words, many written on the spot to a time limit, to act as inspiration for others. And those who have polished their workshop-inspired pieces for inclusion to show what can happen. And who have offered endorsement quotes! What did I do to deserve working with you lovely lot? In order of appearance:

Frances Hay, Lottie Clark, Tessa Bide, Roberta Beary, Sarah Oakes, Diana Wallsgrove, Andy Thomsen, Trudi Taylor, Jo Russ, Liz Churchill, Jane Dunster, Sylvia Petter, Maria Sanger, Dev Jaffe, Ali McGrane, Tim Love, Rosie Mowatt, David Lloyd, Wendy Ogden, Julie Reid, Caro Johnson, Martyn Sands, Alice Wakefield.

Those organisations which have invited me to run writing workshops, and which are mentioned in this book: The Arvon Foundation, Gladstone's Library, The Flash Fiction Festival, Petersfield Museum.

My teaching buddy and co-conspirator in our teaching vehicle, Writing Mill, Cynan Jones, and our indispensible right hand man, David Lloyd. Without Writing Mill, Grist to the Mill sessions would not have been invented, and this book might not exist. Check us out here: www.writingmill.net:

Writers who have inspired some of these games: David Gaffney, Franz Kafka, Dean Atta, Tania Hershman, Electra Rhodes, Karen Blomain, Zoe King, Pascale Petit, George Saunders, Sophy Roberts. And glass artist Elizabeth Lamont.

Proofreader Jo Mortimer https://www.jomortimerproofreader.com/

The team at Ad Hoc Fiction.

Thank you for reading.

And thank you for writing.

VANESSA GEBBIE

Vanessa has won awards for fiction, non fiction and poetry. She is the Welsh author of a constantly growing number of diverse books including

one novel, five collections of short form fictions and two poetry collections. Her novel, *The Coward's Tale* (Bloomsbury) was a Financial Times Novel of the Year. Her latest publication is a translation into German of her illustrated novella in flash, *Ed's Wife and Other Creatures.*

She is an experienced teacher, facilitator and mentor and is contributing editor of *Short Circuit: Guide to the Art of the Short Story* (Salt Publishing, editions i and ii). She is one half of Writing Mill partnership, with the writer Cynan Jones and runs the Grist to the Mill online creative evenings for writers. Her own writing has been used in iGCSE papers, on the High School English curriculum in the USA, has been commissioned by BBC Radio, for anthologies, and is translated into several languages.

She has been invited to tutor for the Arvon Foundation, New Writing South, Spread the Word, The Word Factory, Gladstone's Library and literary events and festivals in the UK and abroad, schools and colleges.

Her creative work has been supported by the Arts Council, by residencies at Gladstone's Library in the UK and Anam Cara Writers and Artists' Retreat in Ireland, and by a Hawthornden Fellowship.

www.vanessagebbie.com

Twitter @vanessagebbie

Instagram @vanessageb

BLANK PAGE FOR YOUR WRITING